CONTENTS

SECTION 1

making Friends

Jamie always had a crowd around her. She wasn't especially knock-out gorgeous. She usually had a couple of zits, and she wasn't exceptionally good at sports.

But she was one of the most popular students at school. Everyone loved her!

Jamie was like a magnet. Wherever she went, someone wanted to be with her. It wasn't unusual for Jamie to be seen listening to one of the football players share a problem with her, or to see her showing a new student how to get to the biology lab.

Why? What was it about Jamie that made everyone notice her? If her looks and her talents weren't anything to brag about, what *did* she have going for her? Here it is—short and simple—Jamie had learned the secret of being popular. She knew how to make friends and keep them.

You already know this book is about helping your friends who are struggling with hurt, confusion and a variety of problems. But guess what? In order for you to be a helping friend, you first have to *have* friends and be the kind of friend others *want* in their lives.

So before we actually get into how you can *help* your friends, let's first take a peek at how you *get* friends and *become* a friend, okay?

(This next stuff is going to be pretty basic. In fact, you may already know it all and can help me write my next book. If you don't need this part, feel free to totally skip it and flip to the very end of this section—page 17.)

the secret

Jamie's secret to popularity really isn't something a rocket scientist has to figure out. It's actually very basic:
JAMIE WAS NICE TO EVERYONE!
Wait a sec, you're thinking. *That's too easy. There's gotta be more to popularity than that!*

Yeah, there are a few more strategies we'll talk about in a few seconds, but the biggest secret of all—the one thousands of teens try to skip over—is simply being nice to *everyone*.

Jamie was as kind to the new student who had no friends at all as she was the football player. She had friends in the band and friends in drama. She refused to only associate with one group of people. Because she was kind to everyone, people responded by wanting to be around her.

there's more

Okay, as mentioned a few lines earlier, there *are* some additional strategies that go along with Jamie's big secret of being nice to everyone. Ready to tackle them? Let's take a few minutes on each one.

SENSATIONAL SMILE.
There's something intriguing about someone who smiles a lot, isn't there? We're automatically drawn to someone who's happy. And wearing a smile usually implies that the person behind it is approachable.

If people know you're approachable, they'll start coming to you. And how will they know? Well, you'll make them feel at ease; comfortable. And how does *that* happen? By smiling. A smile is an open invitation to be approached. It says, "You can talk to me. I'll be friendly with you. Really. It's okay. I'm not going to hurt you."

Smiles also convey something else that's really important when making friends. A smiling person insinuates confidence. (That was really a great point, did you get it? Or did you just zoom by it quickly? Well, to make sure you get it, let's go over it again, K?)

Repeat after me:

SMILING INSINUATES CONFIDENCE.

I can already hear your thoughts screaming through the page at me: *But I'm NOT confident, Susie. I feel insecure, and I'm always worried about what I look like and what everyone else is thinking, and—*

Whoa. Go grab some lemonade from the fridge and cool off. I said *insinuates* not *proves*. In other words, a smile *suggests* that you're confident. You don't have to actually *feel* confident to smile. But when you *do*, people will *think* you're confident. Cool, huh? (Watch the lemonade. You're starting to drip.)

But here's something even cooler: The longer you practice smiling— even in intimidating situations—the sooner your smile will catch up with you. In other words, you'll start to believe what the smile stands for.

> "The Lord would speak to Moses face to face, as a man speaks with his FRIEND"
> (Exodus 33:11).

You'll gain confidence from smiling! No, it won't happen overnight, but it *will* happen. I promise.

Let me introduce you to 16-year-old Jenny. I met Jenny along with 300 other teen girls that I took to Brazil with me on a two-week missions trip. On the final night of the trip, several girls stepped up to the microphone and shared what God had taught them during the past few days.

I'll never forget Jenny. Smiling from ear to ear, she shared her story. "When I was 11," she began, "I was in a terrible car accident. My bottom teeth were knocked out—causing my mouth to be disfigured. I struggled a lot with having a low self-esteem, thinking I was ugly. But you know what? God has shown me that I have a beautiful smile! And my smile is something I can give to everyone I meet. Because He can use my smile to minister to others and to encourage those around me, I no longer have to worry about my outer appearance. God is using my smile!"

Wow. Jenny had learned the secret of flashing a sensational smile. And she was right! God *was* using her smile. Jenny always had a crowd of people around her. She was approachable, easy to talk to, and she genuinely cared about others. Know what else? She was beginning to *feel* the confidence that her smile *suggested!*

What about you? Will you make a point to start working right now on developing a sensational smile? Just for fun . . . since you've already dripped lemonade all over this page anyway . . . I'll leave some space here for you to doodle on. Know what I want you to doodle? Smiles. Make as many as you want. Big ones. Little ones. Funny ones. Magnetic ones. Create a million smiles right here, and I'll go grab a Cherry 7-Up and meet you on the next page.

doodle area

Let's recap, okay? Jamie was popular because:

1. She was nice to everyone.
2. She smiled a lot.

Ready for the next one? Jamie knew how to talk *and* listen. It wasn't unusual at all to see her listening to someone sharing a problem, but she was also a good conversationalist. In other words, the other person didn't have to do all the talking.

Everyone knows someone who talks all the time. They're not much fun to be around, are they? I once had a friend whom I went out to eat a lot with. She talked all the time. As in nonstop. Once in a while, she'd say, "Susie, I don't understand you. You travel all over the place and speak to thousands of teenagers every year, but you sure don't say much one-on-one."

I *wanted* to say, "How can I? You never give me a chance!"

Everyone wants to talk. We all have a story to tell. Each of us enjoy having someone listen to what we say. It makes us feel important when someone is truly interested in what we're saying.

LEARN TO LISTEN.
When other people find out you're willing to listen, believe me, they'll talk—and they'll be talking to *you!* But when you listen . . . *really* listen. I'm talking about genuine listening—not the kind of "listening" where you focus your eyes on the person speaking, but your mind is focused on Jason Issacs who's approaching your table.

When someone is talking to you, zero in 100 percent on *that person.* It's easy to tell when someone's just pretending to listen but really thinking about something else. That won't fly in making friends. You'll be known as a phony.

Okay, but once I've learned to be a great listener, what am I going to do with all the stuff I'm hearing? Oooh. That's a good one.

You're going to have to learn to keep secrets. A genuine friend is one who can be trusted. When Josh tells you in confidence that he likes Bethany, you can't run off and tell her—even though it'll kill you not to.

Would it ever be right to break a secret? Oooh. Another good one. And the answer is yes. If your friend is in danger of hurting herself or someone else, you can't keep that information private. But we'll talk more about that later when we get into how to help your friends who are going through really rough times.

Back to keeping secrets. Make it a priority. When people realize they can trust you—truly trust you—they'll feel safe in open-

ing up to you with their problems, hurts, questions, fears and dreams. But listening is only half of this strategy. It's just as important to *talk* as it is to listen. The key is learning *when* to talk. Try not to talk just to hear yourself talking—that brings us back to my friend who just talked and talked and talked allllll the time. No one else could get a word in edgewise.

Don't put the burden of the entire conversation on someone else. You've got to do your part, too. Talking is learning how to be a good conversationalist.

Seventeen-year-old Lance says, "It always freaks me out when I'm with a girl who expects me to do all the talking. That's too much pressure. I like being with girls who can hold their own end of the conversation."

Jeremy feels the same way: "Sometimes I'll be with a girl who acts like she's afraid to say something. I mean, how else are we gonna get to know each other if we don't talk and listen? But sometimes girls act like what they have to say isn't important. Of course it is! I wouldn't be spending time with a girl, trying to carry on a conversation with her, if I didn't care about what she has to say."

Guess what? Lance and Jeremy aren't the only ones who feel this way. Everyone wants to be in a friendship that has both give and take when it comes to talking.

Yeah, but sometimes I just don't know what to say!

I hear you. And I understand. Here's a little secret: If you're really listening to what the other person is saying, you can ask questions about what he's talking about.

Eric just mentioned he has a lot of math homework. So make a question out of what you've heard: "Do you like math?"

"Ah, it's okay. But Mrs. Johnson sure gives us a lot of homework!"

Now grab your next question from what he's just told you.

"I haven't had Mrs. Johnson. Is she a good teacher? Does she explain things well?"

Of course, you don't always have to continue the conversation by asking questions. Throw your own thoughts out there as well. Again, Eric has just mentioned he has a lot of math homework. You contribute your own thoughts: "I don't have any math homework, but I've got a huge report to write on this play called 'Our Town' that we've been reading in Lit."

Yeah, okay. But Eric and I already know each other. How do I get a conversation going with someone I don't know at all, or someone I know—but not really well?

Another good question. Will you help me write my next book? I like you!

Asking questions is the best way to get a conversation going. Even if you know the person really well—you're already good friends—asking questions will help you get to know them even better.

About a year ago, I went on a safari in Kenya, Africa with a friend of mine. Knowing it was going to be a looooong flight from Colorado Springs to Nairobi, Kenya, I took one of my favorite books along: *The Book of Questions.*

Even though we were already great friends (after all, we were traveling across the world together!), we still had a blast asking fun questions and learning more about each other from our answers.

Since I love questions so much, I decided to create a list of my own to use when the need arises. I'll share them with you, and you can try them out on friends, acquaintances and even people you don't know yet. I'll give you 25 questions, and I'll leave some space for you to create five of your own to add to the list, okay? Here goes:

- If you had to give up one of your five senses (sight, hearing, taste, touch, smell), which would you choose to live without?
- If you suddenly won a million dollars, how would you spend it?
- If you could receive truthful answers to any two questions, *what* would you ask and to *whom* would you ask it?
- How would you react if a stranger approached you and offered to carry your groceries to the car?
- Is it always wrong to kill? What about insects? Animals?
- If you could be a contestant on any TV game show, which would you choose?
- If you had to live in one of these places, which would you choose: Antarctica or Siberia?
- Would you be willing to have superfrightening dreams every night for three years if it meant you'd be really popular the rest of your life?
- Do you think there's life on other planets?
- If *you* were Eve, would *you* have eaten the forbidden fruit?
- If *you* were Adam, would *you* have blamed it on *Eve?*
- If you could invent a brand-new chewing gum, what would you call it? How would it differ from all other gum on the market? What flavor would it be?

- What's the most frightening thing that's ever happened to you so far?
- Do you think anyone ever cleans out water towers? If you were offered a job working on top of and inside a water tower, what fears, questions or doubts would you have?
- What's the most valuable thing you own?
- What's one thing your parents were right about after all?
- What makes you laugh uncontrollably?
- What would you be more frightened of, a snake, a lion or a tarantula?
- What's your favorite color?
- If you had to choose between TV and radio, which would you do without for an entire year?
- What's the difference between encouraging someone and complimenting someone?
- If you could write a book, what would you title it? What would it be about? How much would you sell it for?
- What's the most recent book you've read?
- What classes in school do you think will be completely useless to you in the future?
- What's the most exciting thing going on in your life *right now?*

Okay, it's your turn! Think of five more questions and jot them here in the space provided.

1. _____

2. _____

3. _____

4. _____

5. _____

Recap—Popularity is gained through:
1. Being nice to everyone.
2. Smiling a lot.
3. Knowing how to talk *and* listen.
And here's the next one:

NEVER BE A KNOW-IT-ALL.

Let's face it. Unless you're a direct relative of Albert Einstein, you probably don't know everything. But I'll bet you know a few teens who *act* like they know it all, don't you?

No one enjoys being around a know-it-all . . . especially when you really *don't* know it all! So don't try to act like it.

Heather always had a better story. Whenever someone talked about their family vacation, Heather piped up with a better vacation. And when someone told a joke, Heather always tried to outdo it with a funnier joke.

When someone asked Heather a question, she'd always give them an answer—even when she didn't know the answer! It wasn't long before people stopped asking for her opinion about things. They got tired of being around her. She was a know-it-all.

Why do people like Heather act that like? Why are they always trying to outdo someone else's story or try to make others think they know it all?

Insecurity. Insecurity. Insecurity.

Either you really *do* know a lot and just like to show off so you can be the center of attention (which means you're insecure), or you really *don't* know it all, but you want to make people *think* you do, because you're afraid if they think you *don't* know everything, they won't like you (which means you're insecure).

Guess what? You don't have to be the center of attention! It's really okay to blend in. You don't always have to the star—the one who's right—the one who has the best story.

Nor do you always have to have the answer. If people befriend you simply because of your knowledge, they're not real friends anyway. If you have a friend who falls into this know-it-all category, you can help her climb out by letting her know that she doesn't have to earn your friendship.

If *you're* the one in the know-it-all division, allow God to help you move from the spotlight of attention to focusing on the needs of others. Humility is extremely attractive. Ask God to help you become humble.

In fact, why wait? Let's pray about it right now.

> **Dear Jesus,**
>
> I confess I've done some not-so-nice things to be the center of attention. I've interrupted. I've made up stories. I've talked loud. I've bragged about stuff.
>
> Will You forgive me, Father? I don't want to be insecure and always fighting for attention. I want to be like You— humble yet confident. Interested in others yet willing to share myself with people.
>
> Teach me how to be humble, Jesus. Thank You.
>
> In Your name I pray, Amen.

Want to stay on the right track? Here's a terrific Scripture verse to memorize: "Do not think of yourself more highly than you ought, but rather think of yourself with sober judgment, in accordance with the measure of faith God has given you" (Romans 12:2-3).

there's still more

Okay, it's recap time again. Popularity is gained through:
1. Being nice to everyone.
2. Smiling a lot.
3. Knowing how to talk *and* listen.
4. Not being a know-it-all.
And the next strategy for making friends?
BE YOURSELF.

Tawni was really frustrated! Hannah's dad was totally rich, and almost every week Hannah arrived at school wearing superexpensive stuff—like jeans that cost $100 or a jacket for $350 or new shoes that were easily $200.

Tawni couldn't keep up. Even though most of the girls tried to imitate what Hannah did and wore, Tawni had had enough. Instead of being a follower, she finally decided to simply be herself. To set her own trends. To stop focusing on what others were doing.

So one Saturday, she and her mom went thrift-store shopping. Tawni only had $20 saved from baby-sitting, but it turned out, that was all she needed! She got a whole stash of great stuff.

When they got home, her mom helped her customize it just for her. They cut the jeans into below-the-knee capri style, and sewed funky patches on both legs.

They mixed and matched a few of her other purchases, and they created a totally-cool hat out of something no one would have guessed had any more life to it. Tawni got a weird-looking pair of shoes for $2—which was great, because she liked weird stuff—and with the help of her mom, put together a brand-new outfit.

Yeah, people looked at her on Monday morning when she walked into school. Especially Hannah. "Tawni! I love it! Oh, Mylanta! I've got to have it. Please take me shopping with you next week!"

You guessed it. It wasn't long before thrift-store shopping became the "in" thing to do. By deciding to simply be herself, Tawni had become a trend-setter.

What about you? Are you being *you*, or are you simply trying to imitate everyone else? God created you in His image. He has made you unique and special. He doesn't want you copy-catting those around you. He wants you to be *you*—the way He created you.

Oftentimes, people who try to imitate others do so because they're afraid to be themselves. Check *this* out: "Fear not, for I have redeemed you; I have called you by name; you are mine" (Isaiah 43:1).

That's terrific ammunition for eliminating fear. If God Himself chooses us, redeems us and calls us by our name, what do we have to fear? When we truly realize that the King of Kings accepts us and loves us just as we are, that sets us free from having to impress others, imitate others or follow others.

there's still more

Ready for the recap? Popularity is gained through:
1. Being nice to everyone.
2. Smiling a lot.
3. Knowing how to talk *and* listen.
4. Not being a know-it-all.
 5. Being yourself.
And . . . drum roll please . . . ready? Here's the next one:
ADD VALUE TO THOSE AROUND YOU.
Carrie Bobb, like Jamie, always has a crowd of people around her. She's 21 now, but since she was in junior high, she's always been one of the most popular students in school. Now, as she's completing her college education, once again, she's one of the most popular people on campus.

I pulled Carrie aside and asked what her secret was: "I have a list of 20 things I try to do every day," she said. "There are some things on the list that change and fluctuate, but there are a few things that remain the same."

"Give me an example of something that remains the same— something you try to do every single day," I said.

"Okay. Well, I try really hard to add value to those around me."

"Every day?" I questioned.

"Every day," she said. "People light up when you recognize something they do well and let them know it. It only takes a minute to give someone a compliment or to notice what gifts a person has. So why not bring it to attention? It automatically adds value to how they see themselves. I want to be the kind of person that's always seeing the positive attributes in others. I don't ever want to tear someone down. When Jesus walked the earth, He affirmed and encouraged. I want to do that, too. I want to build people up."

I decided to hang out with her a couple of weeks and watch her in action. It was true! Carrie *daily* brought worth to those around her by noticing the good in their lives.

She complimented our bus driver. She sat with a teen girl who was confused about her boyfriend, and Carrie affirmed the girl's willingness to obey God—even if it meant breaking up with the guy.

Carrie told Brett she saw a real depth about him. She told Matt it was cool to see him using his musical gifts to glorify the Lord. She noticed that Nikki was not only great with large groups of people but that she was also terrific one-on-one, and Carrie let her know. The list goes on and on. Genuinely, Carrie affirms those around her adding value to their lives.

Will you determine to do the same? Find something good in each of your family members and encourage them with it. Look for people who go the extra mile for others, and tell them you notice. Watch those who are shy and highlight their tender spirits. You'll find it's amazing to see people actually light up when you affirm them and add value to what they're already doing well!

Following those six strategies really *will* help you make friends. Let's recap one more time—I want to make sure you don't forget!

Popularity is gained through:

1. Being nice to everyone.
2. Smiling a lot.
3. Knowing how to talk *and* listen.
4. Not being a know-it-all.
5. Being yourself.
6. Adding value to those around you.

but there's still more

Even though those six secrets will help you develop good friendships, there's still something reallyreallyreally important I've gotta tell you.

Wait a sec! You said that was it. You said if I followed these six strategies, I'd learn how to make friends. How can there be more?

Believe it or not, there really IS more. And this is of upmost importance. Totally significant. Extremely noteworthy. Like your top priority.

All right already. What is it?

Before I tell you what it is, I need to be honest with you: This last item may not help you make friends. In fact, you might even *lose* a few. But it is THE most important thing you'll ever do in your life. Here it is:

BE JESUS TO THOSE AROUND YOU.

Since Jesus isn't here in the flesh, He's depending on us to be His hands, feet, arms, ears. Are you using your hands, feet, arms and ears to bring glory to Him? What about the rest of you? Are your eyes seeing people as Jesus sees them? Does your mouth speak words of encouragement as Jesus would? Is your voice singing praises to His name?

Are you going the extra mile for someone who needs you? (That's what the rest of this book is about—so we need to get this part settled right now.) *Jesus always loved.* He calls you to do the same. When your friends are hurting, love them. When Juli battles an eating disorder, love her. When Brooke shares that she's been abused, love her. When Geoff confides that his parents are splitting, be Jesus to him. Austin tells you that his mother is dying of cancer. He doesn't need a bunch of philosophical words from you—He needs you to reflect the love of Jesus to him.

Sometimes Jesus loved with "tough love." In other words, He never made excuses for people's sin. He never said, "Well, that's okay. You didn't mean to." He allowed people to feel guilty for the disobedience in their lives, but He continued to love them.

You do the same. And when your friends are battling deep scars, don't allow them to make excuses. Love them like Jesus would. Sometimes that means giving a hug. Sometimes it means telling them something they don't want to hear, like: "I'll be here for you, but you've got to go ask him to forgive you." Or "I'll go with you, but you really need to see a counselor."

Being Jesus to your friends may not be easy, because Jesus didn't always do the popular thing—He always did the *right* thing. And sometimes doing what's right may cost you some friends.

Being Jesus means being willing to be a servant. Jesus told His disciples to serve—wash each other's feet. And to set the example, He knelt before them and washed *their* feet. Imagine! The creator of the universe washing feet! (See John 13:1-17 for the whole story.)

Washing feet can get stinky. It's uncomfortable. It's not easy. But it's right. I had taken a group of teens on a missions trip to South America. During the middle of the trip, I gave a devotion on how Jesus has called us to be servants. I called someone up front and knelt in front of him and washed his feet. Then we divided into small groups and began to wash each other's feet.

One group went left the room and went outside for more privacy. As they were washing each other's feet, a national military man walked by. Without hardly thinking, Jarod politely stopped him and motioned for the officer to sit on the ground with them.

A couple of teens from the group gently untied the man's shoes. One of the girls picked up his feet and placed them in the basin of water. Jarod began washing. Calvin grabbed the towel and tenderly dried the officer's feet.

One by one, they began sharing the difference Christ had made in their lives. When they had finished, the military officer was asking how he could know Jesus like they did. He prayed and surrendered his life to Jesus.

Why? Because a great evangelist had come to town? No. Because of a dazzling Christian concert with flashing lights and smoke machines? No. Simply because a group of teens were determined to reach out and be Jesus to him.

God isn't asking you to be flashy. He may or may not provide you with a stage or a microphone. But He is calling you to serve. To reach out. To be His hands to those around you. To be Him to a lost and dying world.

Will you do it? Even when it's tough? When you're wanting to help your friends come out on top of their problems, the very *best* thing you can do is to be Jesus to them.

"GOD ISN'T ASKING YOU TO BE FLASHY. HE MAY OR MAY NOT PROVIDE YOU WITH A STAGE OR A MICROPHONE. BUT HIE IS CALLING YOU TO SERVE."

Before we really get in to *how* you can help your friends, take a break for a few seconds and take this quiz to help assess what kind of friend you *are*, okay?

QUIZ: What Kind of Friend Are You?
Find out if you're all you can be for your buds
by Jennifer Ellis Freeman

Friendship can be one of the best things in life. It's great to have someone to laugh with during the good times, and it's nice to have a shoulder to cry on during those not-so-good times. There are all kinds of qualities that go into a good friend. How many of them do you have? Take this quiz to see how you stack up as a friend.

1. You're talking to someone at your locker when you see your friend approaching. She's sporting a new hairdo that is a definite don't. The person you're with makes a nasty comment. You
   a. announce that you think the style is great and then study it until you find something about it that you really do like.
   b. ignore the comment and find a time to gently break it to your friend that she might want to try some thing else.
   c. agree with the comment. After all, the style is awful.

2. The party invitation you've been waiting for finally arrives. You are so excited that you immediately call your friend to see what she's going to wear. But when she answers the phone, she tells you she wasn't invited. You
   a. tell her that if she isn't going, you aren't going. You make plans to see a movie together instead.
   b. call the person giving the party and ask if you can bring your friend.
   c. tell her that if she isn't going, you aren't going, but then go anyway.

3. You find out that your friend has seriously let you down. She calls you to apologize. You
   a. forgive her. We've all done some stupid things.
   b. tell her it's okay, but then never trust her again.
   c. slam down the phone and think of a rumor to spread about her the next day.
4. Your friend wants to go on a date, but her mom says no. She asks you to tell her mom that she's with you while she goes on the date. You
   a. tell her you're sorry, but you're not going to lie for her. Instead, help her think of ways she might be able to compromise with her mom.
   b. tell her you'll do it, but just this once.
   c. cover for her. The argument is between her and her mother. You're only helping a friend.

5. Your friend has volunteered to make cookies for the Spring Fling party, but she waits until the last minute. She calls you begging for help. You hate baking. You
   a. give up your Saturday plans and prepare to be covered in flour.
   b. show up on her doorstep with 14 boxes of cookies from the bakery. Tell her all she has to do is put them on a plate and no one will know she didn't make them herself.
   c. tell her you'd help, but you have to walk your dog— all day.

6. At lunch, someone begins to tell a juicy rumor about your friend. You
   a. tell the person talking that you're not going to listen to gossip, especially if it involves someone you care about.
   b. listen to the rumor and then call your friend to see if it's true.
   c. listen to the rumor, call someone else to tell her the rumor and ask if she thinks it's true.

7. You find out your friend has become involved with drugs. You confront her about it, and she tells you to mind your own business. You
   a. immediately tell her parents, a teacher or a school counselor.
   b. let her know how you feel about what she's doing. Make it clear that you care about her, but you won't be around her when she's hurting herself.
   c. let it go. She can make her own decisions.

SCORING:
   If you answered . . .

Mostly A's: You're a truly terrific friend. You know what it means to be a good friend, and you do your best to live up to that. Even when the right choice is not the easy choice, you still come through. Your friends should feel fortunate to have you in their lives.

Mostly B's: You *do* care about your friends, and you usually make good decisions about your friendships. Sometimes, though, you're swayed to make choices that might not be for the best. Think carefully about what it means to be a good friend, and then make sure you stick to it. You and your friends will all be better off.

Mostly C's: You're walking on thin ice with your friendships. If you don't want to fall through, you're going to have to make some changes. Start by making a list of qualities you'd like to see in your own friends. Then make an effort to be that way yourself.

And now we're getting down to why you bought this book—you *do* want to help your friends. They're hurting. Some of them are struggling with a heaviness that's almost beyond description. Let's help them, okay? Being Jesus to them will have eternal effects! Turn the page. It's time to start.

SECTION 2

how to Help your hurting friend

helping a friend
through an Eating
Disorder

Laura's dieting had become much more than important. It had grown into a full-fledged obsession.

I asked her to share her story with you so that you can understand a little better what may be going through the mind of a friend who's struggling with an eating disorder.

Fighting the Food Phantom
by Laura Johnson, R.D./L.D.
as told to Tracy Pullen, R.D./L.D.

Why?
Why did I scarf all that stuff?
A medium pizza, three doughnuts,
two large bowls of ice cream, Chinese food,
four pieces of cinnamon toast. . . .
What made me do it?
Now it's all in my stomach . . .
bloating my body like a balloon.
I've got to get rid of it.
I'll make myself throw up.
Then I'll take some strong laxatives.
One more time I'll rid myself
of everything inside.
Tomorrow WILL be a new day.
Surely, after THIS binge,
my nightmare will stop. . . .
Or will it?

I was the victim of a deadly eating disorder known as bulimia. For 10 years it raged out of control in my life like a flaming inferno—sending me on frequent eating rampages.

I'd swallow everything I could get my hands on. Then, when my belly was painfully swollen, I'd make my way to the nearest rest room.

My horrible bulimic nightmare began during my sophomore year of high school. But the roots stemmed much deeper . . . way back to junior high and my struggles with a tough home life and a poor self-image.

I felt so awkward and ugly back then. My tall frame was undeveloped, and my straight red hair hung limply across my shoulders.

Why didn't I have any friends? Was it because I wore no makeup? I felt like the campus alien with my fair-skinned complexion. All the other kids were trim, tan and trendy. They wore sharp clothes and had all the flashy accessories to go with the latest styles.

surface solution

When high school rolled around, I'd finally had enough. I got so tired of feeling like an outcast that I vowed to make a complete change during Christmas break of my sophomore year. I got my hair cut and styled, had my "colors" done, started using makeup and hit the campus a new woman.

"Laura—is that YOU?" my girlfriends exclaimed.

"WOW . . . where have you been all our lives?" guys would ask. (The same ones who never gave me the time of day before.)

It suddenly felt good to have people notice me—especially the boys! I loved all the attention, and knew I was actually a very attractive young lady.

I also increased my school activities and determined to become more involved. I joined the band, played basketball, softball and competed on the track team.

Mom was thrilled that I was finally coming out of my shell. Especially since things were so messed up at home.

torn on the inside

Dad was an alcoholic, impossible to live with at times. Whenever stuff bugged him, he'd turn to a bottle for relief. Then he'd take his anger out at us. I was sick of tip-toeing around on egg shells . . . but Mom insisted we keep a tight lip on our family secret.

Eventually, she started living out her life through me. I guess Mom wanted her daughter to experience some of the things she missed in life. So she pushed me to excel.

"Whatever you do, give it your absolute best," she'd tell me. So I pasted a smile on my face and vowed to work harder at everything—popularity, high grades, achieving a stunning appearance. If my performance wasn't perfect, it wasn't acceptable.

But this double life was draining. Pushing myself to be perfect in public, then facing the pain at home tore me up inside. Especially seeing my dad drunk—and my mom crushed.

"We can't go on like this," I'd tell Mom. "Dad needs help!"

"This is a private family matter," Mom would say.

My lips were sealed, by my heart ached.

the secret to slender?

Despite the hard times at home, things really seemed to click at school.

I was thrilled to learn toward the end of my junior year that the faculty and administration had selected me to represent our student body at a prestigious and fun leadership conference. Girls from all over the state of Oklahoma would be attending, and I'd have a chance not only to make new friends but to develop leadership skills as well.

Attending Girls State seemed like a lifesaver. It meant time away from home and less pressure. Most of all, there was no fear of running into a drunken parent.

During the week, however, I couldn't help noticing how much my roommates were eating. They were chowing down on all my faves—hot fudge sundaes, pizza, chips, cookies . . . yet they all had fabulous figures. Toward the end of our stay, a girl named Nancy filled me in on their secret.

"We can eat anything we want. It's easy, Laura. After you're finished just go to the bathroom and make yourself throw up."

The idea repulsed me at first, but I so desperately wanted to maintain a good figure—and the thought of never having to skip a meal again to lose weight sounded great. I accepted her suggestion.

> Pushing myself to be perfect in public, then facing the pain at home tore me up inside. Especially seeing my dad drunk—and my mom crushed.

Forcing my finger down my throat seemed weird, but after I threw up the first time, I thought, Hey, this isn't so bad. And it actually works!

I did it a second time, then a third. Before I knew it, I was purging my food on a regular basis. But that was only the beginning.

the raging battle

Through time, I learned what foods I could eat a lot of and throw up easily. Ice cream was one of them, so I consumed large quantities of the creamy sweet stuff. Soon, I started taking several laxatives every day—along with throwing up—to hasten the process.

Weeks merged into years and my once simple key to a knockout bod turned into an out-of-control obsession. I found myself waking daily to the same haunting question: Will I be able to eat normally today without throwing up? Can I make it one day without laxatives or diet pills?

But the inferno raged within. It became difficult to sit through English and concentrate on adjectives and adverbs when I was mentally creating an intricate plan of when I would binge and purge next. I spent more than $25 a day on food, consuming between 7,000 and 10,000 calories.

bruised by bulimia

Little did I know that the inside of my body was slowly deteriorating. I knew what I was doing wasn't normal, but at least I had a flat stomach.

Eventually, throwing up everything I ate made me feel terrible about myself, despite my figure. I got to the point where I really wanted to stop . . . but couldn't.

I felt as though I was on a high-speed roller coaster and couldn't get off. I wanted to stop the ride, but I knew I'd have to do it myself. The thought of others finding out that I had this big problem—and that I wasn't perfect—literally terrified me.

I began my own private search for a cure. I attended seminars on eating disorders, read books, studied nutrition and eventually became a registered dietitian.

If I can just learn all the proper information about food and place myself on the right diet, I told myself, I'll be able to eat normally and the nightmare will be over.

It didn't work. As a professional nutritionist, I easily put others on diets but couldn't make one work for myself. I felt like I had fallen into a deep, black hole and couldn't climb out. No light. No hope. No answers.

Then he came along. Bryce . . . the man of my dreams. He seemed too good to be true. He was everything I ever dreamed about in a boyfriend . . . tall, blond, handsome, sensitive.

Bryce and I fell in love. And as our relationship grew, I knew he was the man I wanted to spend the rest of my life with. For the first time ever, I met someone who seemed to love me unconditionally.

But would he still love me if he knew about my secret? I often wondered as he wrapped his strong arms around me.

We just couldn't get engaged until I told him about my horrible nightmare. At the same time, though, I didn't want him to know.

In desperation, I went to a counselor named Dr. Morris.

"Doctor, I've been bulimic for 10 years," I told him as I entered his office. "I need help. I can't go on like this."

He rubbed his chin and smiled warmly. "Laura, I'm glad you've come to me. You're facing a problem that can't be handled alone.

"I have a group of people with eating disorders that I meet with weekly for intensive counseling," he continued. "I'd like you to be a part of the group.

My eyes opened wide and a pain shot through my stomach. "No!" I rebelled. "No way, Doctor. I don't want anyone else to know about my problem. Can't the two of us just work it out?"

Dr. Morris reminded me that my bulimia had been a private matter for such a long time that I needed to verbalize with others who were going through the same thing.

I had no other option, and things just had to change . . . so I agreed.

I thought I'd feel some ray of hope when I finally took this dreaded step, but the doctor threw me a real curve ball.

"Do not be afraid, for I AM with you."
(Isaiah 43:5)

"Laura, Bryce needs to know," he said. "I cannot let you join the group until you tell him what's going on."

"That's not fair!" I screamed. "I want to work it out before we get married. He doesn't need to be bothered with this."

Dr. Morris calmly yet firmly held his ground. "Our group therapy will be difficult. You'll need his support. You will not be able to make it on your own. You have to tell him."

I still hesitated, but he continued. "My next group won't begin for two months. That gives you plenty of time."

During the next couple of months I worked up my courage to take another painstaking step: Tell Bryce my ugly secret.

sharing the secret

"Bryce, I have something I need to tell you," I said with a quivering voice. "And I . . . I just don't know how. . . ."

"Laura, . . . you can tell me anything," he said with those kind, puppy-dog eyes.

"I . . . I mean, I have this . . . problem," I hesitated. Tears rolled down my face, so I turned my head and covered my mouth.

"Honey, what is it?"

"I don't want to tell you this ugly thing about myself. You might stop loving me."

"Laura, nothing can ever come between us," he said as he gripped both my shoulders and looked me in the eyes. "I love you and nothing can ever change that."

Bryce was right.

After I revealed my nightmare to him, he held me in his arms and wept—then vowed to help me win this battle. It felt like a ton of boulders had been lifted from my head. And for the first time in my life, I had the hope to continue.

the courage to quit

I then began six months of intensive group therapy. Dr. Morris was right—it was difficult.

The first thing we had to do was remove our symptoms: taking laxatives, throwing up and any other means of getting rid of our food.

Supper was a nightmare. Sometimes it was a two-hour process. We sat around a large table and were required to eat everything on our plate. It was hard . . . considering that this food couldn't be purged.

One particular evening the doctor placed a tray in front of each of us containing one cup of spaghetti, a half cup of green beans and a slice of garlic bread.

My eyes bugged out. I can't eat all of this, I thought. I'll gain weight immediately!

I had been used to consuming probably five times that much—but also getting rid of it. Since I was not allowed to do that anymore, I was terrified of eating an entire meal—even though it contained only 315 calories.

Six months of intensive therapy taught me how to see food in its proper perspective. I know now that for my 5' 7" frame I can consume 1,800 to 2,400 calories per day, and if I exercise about three times a week, I won't gain because my body actually uses the nutrients I consume.

facing the future— with a smile

When my group therapy concluded, I began six months of non-intensive therapy—going beneath the symptoms and learning why I did what I did. This helped me gain self-confidence and a greater ability to deal with the pressures and conflicts of life. One big struggle I tackled was my hard home life—and my messed-up dad.

I began to realize that my drive to be perfect centered on my imperfect dad. I desperately wanted to compensate for the disappointments at home—and sense my own self-worth. So I tried to fill the holes in my life by being the best at everything . . . especially my appearance. That's when bulimia got its hold on me.

Thankfully, I got things in perspective and got out of the deadly cycle. The future finally looks bright—not perfect.

There is a newfound sense of freedom and hope in Laura's life—one which can only be perfected by a personal relationship with Jesus Christ. Laura's search for security was rooted in the desire for unconditional love and acceptance. In 1 John 4:7, the Bible states this love "comes from God."

And check this out: "This is how God showed his love among us: He sent his one and only Son into the world that we might live through him. This is love: not that we loved God, but that he loved us and sent his Son as an atoning sacrifice for our sins" (1 John 4:9-10).

how can you help?

Your friend who is struggling with an eating disorder, may be experimenting with laxatives, diuretics and vomiting—which can all be life-threatening. It's important that you understand the danger so you can share it with your friend.

The Danger of Vomiting

The acid in our stomach is strong enough to eat our skin and tear the enamel off our teeth. Excessive vomiting forces stomach acid into the esophagus, which causes pain and swelling in the throat. After a period of time one runs the risk of not only tearing the throat but rupturing the esophagus as well. Also, the more one vomits, the more scar tissue is built up in the esophagus, causing the throat to narrow. This makes it extremely difficult and painful to swallow.

The Dangers of Laxatives

Laxative abuse (like excessive vomiting) can mess up the body's electrolytes. This means potassium is lost. That's pretty critical because it's vital for our heart to function normally. Without the proper amount of potassium we lose respiratory function. Most anorexics (willfully starving yourself) die from heart failure—this is how it begins.

Karen Carpenter, a popular singer from the '70s, died from heart failure due to anorexia and laxative abuse. She had been released from the hospital and was in recovery when her heart stopped functioning due to the amount of damage that had already been done.

Continued excessive use of laxatives can also cause chronic constipation. There is no medication available that can treat this, because of the total disruption of the body's normal electrical circuit. Our body needs to maintain the balance we were created with. When we cause our insides to become unbalanced, we're tampering with God's intricate and creative wiring system.

The Danger of Diuretics

Diuretics or "water pills" cause the kidneys to secrete larger than normal amounts of urine. This in turn causes an eloctrolyte imbalance and dehydration. Again, an electrolyte imbalance lowers your potassium, which causes heart failure.

If Someone You Know Has an Eating Disorder:

❶ Don't ignore it.

❷ Let your friend know you're aware of the problem.

❸ Let her know there is hope.

❹ Let her know there are treatment programs and counselors who can help.

❺ Don't play "psychologist" . . . you are not in a position to fix or save the person with an eating disorder.

❻ Never impose a moral tone. When we make moral judgments we essentially say that someone is good or bad because of what she does/feels or doesn't do/feel. Examples of moral judgments:

- "Why can't you just push away from the table?"

- "How can you do that to yourself?"

- "If you really cared about your family, you wouldn't do that."

- "You're certainly not living the way God wants you to live."

AN EATING DISORDER IS NOT A MORAL PROBLEM; IT IS AN ADDICTIVE DISORDER.

misconceptions

Your friend battling anorexia or bulimia may have some twisted ideas such as:

1. "If I read the right book(s) I'll find the knowledge I need to recover from my eating disorder."

2. "I have to figure out a way to deal with this problem on my own; everyone else will think I'm a horrible person if they find out what I do or what I think."

3. "If I find the right diet (or nutritional information), I'll be able to give up my eating disorder.

4. "If I can just get down to a certain weight, everything will be okay."

5. "I'll eventually outgrow this. I'm just going through a phase right now."

If you hear any of the above rationales from your friend, please lovingly, but firmly, tell her she deceiving herself. Encourage her to seek professional help. Volunteer to go with her, if that will help.

Here's a simple checklist to go through with your friend. Of course, this isn't the final word on eating disorders, but there's a possibility that if she checks several of the first 11 statements, she has an eating disorder. Even if she checks many of the statements, there's an excellent chance she has an eating disorder.

- ❑ I cannot control my eating.
- ❑ I weigh several times a day.
- ❑ I feel that if I could control my weight, everything else in my life would be great.
- ❑ I'm overly controlled about my eating.
- ❑ I avoid being around other people when I am feeling fat.
- ❑ I have difficulty eating in front of other people, or I have trouble eating what I would like to eat when I am with others.
- ❑ I exercise to make up for what I have eaten.
- ❑ I usually eat for reasons other than hunger.
- ❑ I take laxatives or diuretics to make up for what I have eaten.
- ❑ I hide food.
- ❑ If I can't eat perfectly, I might as well not follow a diet.
- ❑ I will go to great lengths to avoid conflict.
- ❑ I take care of everyone but me.
- ❑ I am a people pleaser.
- ❑ I feel good knowing I am a perfectionist.
- ❑ I often feel guilty or ashamed.
- ❑ I deliberately stay very busy and am always in a hurry.
- ❑ No one person really knows everything about me.
- ❑ I find it hard to ask for help.
- ❑ I am just existing.
- ❑ I feel totally out of control.
- ❑ Most people have no idea what I am feeling.

"Jesus was a FRIEND of sinners."
(Matthew 11:19)

If your friend checked several of the above statements, she probably finds it extremely difficult to separate her self-esteem from her weight and from what the scale says.

Let her know that you love her *no matter what she weighs!* Give her lots of hugs and bathe her in prayer!

I'm going to include a fiction story here that really captures the pressure of wanting to fit in with the right look and size. Please share it with your friend, okay?

Middle of the Road Megan
The cost of popularity can be high.
How much is Megan willing to pay?
by Heather Klassen

"We sit here, Megan," Jillian said, steering me toward an already crowded table. I didn't mind having to squeeze in. I felt only gratitude to Jillian for taking pity on me, the new girl. Since homeroom, she'd helped me navigate the halls to my classrooms and even waited outside my last class before lunch. Now here I sat, already being accepted into Jillian's group. I smiled as Jillian introduced me around the table.

"So you're new," the girl across from me said. We had just been introduced, so I managed to remember her name, Vanessa.

After a few minutes of observation, I knew I wouldn't forget her name, either. I could tell Vanessa was popular. She easily flirted with the boys who stopped to talk to her, flashing those huge, dark eyes and flipping her thick, dark hair over her shoulders.

The other girls at the table listened when she spoke, laughed when she laughed, and seemed to agree with her about everything. Vanessa was beautiful and popular.

And I was sitting with her on my first day at a new school.

I couldn't believe my luck. At my old school I'd never been *un*popular, but I definitely wasn't considered one of the popular kids. I just acted friendly to everyone, and everyone was friendly in response. Middle of the Road Megan, that's always been me.

"In" Equals Thin

"Yes, I am," I replied to Vanessa's statement. Digging into my backpack, I pulled out my lunch. As I set the food in front of me, I felt Vanessa watching. I looked up.

"You're going to eat all that?" she asked.

"All what?" I looked at my normal-for-me lunch: A turkey sandwich, an apple and two of my dad's butterscotch cookies. Oh, and the milk I forgot to buy. "This is my lunch," I said perplexed. *What else would I do with it, besides eat it?* I wondered.

The table had fallen silent, listening. I glanced around at the other girls, trying to figure out their lunches. One girl munched on a rice cake, another an apple. That was the only evidence of food on the table; every other girl, Vanessa included, had only a can of diet soda in front of her.

"Did you already eat?" I asked, wondering how they possibly could have, since Jillian and I arrived just after the bell.

Vanessa laughed. "Megan, if that's your lunch, that's your business, but personally, I'd rather be sitting *here* than over *there*." Vanessa glanced over at the table next to us.

I looked, too. A table of girls, like us. Laughing, talking. I didn't see any difference, except that there were no boys hanging around them. When Jillian led me to her table, I had been glad to see people from various ethnic groups. *All right,* I had thought, *no prejudice here.*

But as I looked at that table again, and then at ours, I started to see the difference. I sat at a table of thin girls. Some, like Vanessa, very thin. The girls at the other table weren't. A few were really heavy, the rest all different sizes, even what I consider normal. Just not *thin.*

Now I knew what determined if you were in or out at this school. I'd been in high school long enough to know that I had landed with the popular group. I guess Jillian had sized me up, decided I met the criteria, and here I sat. I consider myself normal size, maybe a little on the thin side. Food's really not a problem for me.

But as the bell rang, and the girls at the table stood up, I realized that I was probably borderline for this group. Not at all overweight, but not really *thin* like some of the others. Especially Vanessa, with her impossibly tiny waist and pelvic bones jutting through the front of her jeans.

Weighing the Options

I gathered up the lunch I hadn't had time to eat. *Just as well,* I thought as I stuffed it back into the sack.

 how to Help your hurting friend

"I'll help you find your next class," Jillian offered.

As we passed the garbage cans, I threw my lunch in.

"See ya," Jillian called as I walked into chemistry.

I slid into a seat, dug into my backpack for a pencil, but only found one with a broken tip. I tapped the shoulder of the girl in front of me. She turned around.

"Could I please borrow a pencil?" I asked.

"You're new," the girl said, ignoring my question. "I saw you at lunch with *Vanessa's group.*"

The she said 'Vanessa's group' left no doubt that Vanessa's friends were not her favorite people. The girl was heavy, not friends with Vanessa obviously, and had no plans to lend me a pencil. She turned back around.

My day had started out great, but now I didn't like the direction it was heading. At my old school, as Middle of the Road Megan, I had managed to be, if not friends, then at least friendly with all kinds of people. Tall, short, fat, thin, smart, not so smart. My old school hadn't been perfect, we had cliques too, but somehow *here* the lines seemed much more distinct. No crossing over.

I wanted to be friends with all kinds of people, but I had to admit I really wanted to meet guys. Cute, popular guys. And I could tell which group I needed to belong to for that.

After school, starving, I devoured a pot of soup and half a loaf of bread. I'd never skipped lunch before.

"I'll grab something at school," I told my mom the next morning as she questioned my leaving without lunch.

"Do you have money?"

"Sure," I called back as I headed out. Only a little. Luckily, a can of soda doesn't cost much.

A can of diet soda didn't fill me up. *I'll get used to it,* I figured. *All the girls in my group do it, so it can't be that tough.*

Even after I could find all my classes, Jillian waited for me in the halls. So did Vanessa. And by hanging around them, I managed to hang around with guys, too. Cute, popular guys. Just what I had wanted. It felt great to be in the popular crowd. Of course, half the kids at my new school acted like I didn't exist, and that didn't feel great. It didn't feel like me, Middle of the Road Megan, friendly to everyone, and everyone friendly to me.

My stomach rumbled every afternoon, so when school let out I would charge home and raid the cupboards. I tried to watch it though, and I started weighing myself every day. Couldn't hurt to be careful.

A Heavy Burden to Carry

Vanessa's locker was close to mine, so sometimes I'd catch her there. One day as I approached, Vanessa leaned deep into her locker. She seemed startled when I called her name, and practically jumped out of the locker.

"Hi," she mumbled, wiping her mouth with the back of her hand. "I'm late." She slammed her locker and took off too quickly to see that it didn't close.

The locker door swung open. I reached over to close it, but stopped when I saw the contents of Vanessa's locker. A crumpled bag of potato chips, jumbo size, lay at the bottom. An empty cookie bag rested on top of that, and dozens of candy bar wrappers littered the pile.

I stared, thinking, Food? Vanessa has food in her locker? Or should I say, the remains of food, the crumbs. I shook my head. This didn't make sense. Ultra thin Vanessa never eats. Who ate this food?

I closed Vanessa's locker and headed toward English Lit. Vanessa was in my class. I'd be able to ask her about this.

I took my seat just as the bell rang. No chance to talk to Vanessa. But five minutes into the class, as we worked on compositions, Vanessa asked Mr. Hurd for the bathroom pass and left the room.

I saw my chance to talk to Vanessa privately. I knew Mr. Hurd would say I had to wait until Vanessa returned, so I told him it was kind of an emergency. Not wanting to know the details of my bathroom emergency, he let me go.

As I pushed open the rest room door, I heard a strange sound. Not your typical bathroom noise. I stood still and listened. Someone was throwing up.

"Vanessa?" I called. "Is that you?"

The throwing-up sounds continued. I checked under the stalls until I spotted Vanessa's shoes. We were alone in the rest room. It had to be her.

"Vanessa, are you sick?"

I heard a strangled cry, so I pushed lightly on the stall door. She hadn't locked it.

Vanessa looked up at me from her crouched-over position.

"Are you sick"? I repeated. "Can I help?"

Vanessa shook her head. "I'm not sick," she whispered.

Suddenly it clicked. The empty bags of junk food, the throwing up, the impossible thinness. *Vanessa had bulimia.* We had learned about it in health last year. *Vanessa really was sick.*

"Vanessa, you need help," I said.

She shook her head again. "No, I'm fine. I'm skinny."

"You may be skinny, but you're not fine," I insisted. "There are people you can talk to about this—people who can help."

"I need to be thin," Vanessa replied. "I need to be popular. This works for me."

As I stared at beautiful Vanessa, crouched over a toilet on a not-very-clean floor, I saw her need, and I saw mine, too. Too clearly. What Vanessa was willing to do to be popular! And what I was willing to do; to be hungry, to not care if people thought me unfriendly, to give up *me*, Middle of the Road Megan.

I held out my hand.

"Take my hand, Vanessa," I pleaded. "I'll help you up. Then we'll get you the help you need."

Vanessa stared at my hand. *Take it, Vanessa,* I silently begged. *You need help to get your life back on track. I'm sure you don't need to do this to be popular,* I thought. *And you need help with whatever your other problems are, whatever it is that has led you to being bulimic.*

And me? Well, I don't think I need what I thought I did. After I do this, after I help Vanessa, I'm planning to get back on the right track for me. The one right down the middle.

"Take my hand, Vanessa," I started to say again; but I didn't need to finish. Because she did.

helping a friend
through
Depression

Haley was an outgoing 15-year-old girl who was excited about heading to Latin America with several other teens under my care on a recent missions adventure. Prior to the trip, she had written me about her excitement of sharing Jesus with people in another country.

After a brief two-day training period in Miami, we boarded our all-night flight for our southbound destination. Only then, did we learn that Haley was scared of flying. *Really* scared! She was beside herself—agitated, on-edge and teary-eyed. I couldn't help but wonder why she hadn't bothered to tell anyone about her fear *before* she decided to take the trip.

Nine hours seemed like an eternity with Haley's anxious and fearful spirit. We finally arrived at our destination, made our way to our lodging and unpacked. I had barely put my things away when I noticed Haley sitting in a corner weeping. Not crying lightly—weeping.

I sat on the floor next to her and asked her if she was homesick. She could barely talk through the sobs, but she managed to tell me she was.

"Well, it's okay to be homesick," I said. "I'm glad that you have a family you're so close to that you miss them when you're apart. That's wonderful."

Knowing Haley hadn't really slept the night before, I encouraged her to turn in early and get as much sleep as she could before we headed out for ministry the next day. Haley went to bed, but she didn't get much sleep. Neither did her roommates. Haley kept them awake most of the night with her continuous weeping.

As the trip progressed, Haley's condition worsened. Most teens who are homesick, call home, cry a bit, then get on with their purpose of being in a foreign country. Not Haley.

She called home. A lot. But she wouldn't quit crying. I tried to get her to be specific about why she was crying, but that only confused me more. "Haley, we're only going to be here a week," I said. "You'll be with your family again before you know it."

She continued to sob.

"You can pick up the phone and call home as much as you want," I reminded her. "It's not like you're out of touch with your mom."

She continued to sob.

"Haley, why did you come on this missions trip?"

She continued to sob, but forced a few words through her tears: "I thought God wanted me to."

"Well, I believe He brought you here," I affirmed. "And He has you here for a specific purpose. Will you let Him use you while you're here?"

She continued to sob.

"Haley, why are you crying? I mean, you knew when you came on this missions trip that you'd have to be away from your family for a week and a half and that you'd be out of your comfort zone."

She continued to sob but pushed a few more words out of her mouth. "But I didn't know it was going to be this uncomfortable."

We were staying in a dorm-type atmosphere. I thought it was great. Everyone had a bed, showers, toilets that worked, clean sheets, soap. I had stayed in some remote areas in primitive Third-World villages that made this feel luxurious. I was having trouble identifying with her, but I wanted to help.

"Haley, we're in a great facility, we're safe, we've eaten good food. What's making you uncomfortable?"

"Well, I didn't know I was going to have to sleep on such a small bunk with such a hard, lumpy pillow!"

"Haley," I continued, "you're going to hold orphans in your lap tomorrow that don't even *have* a pillow. You'll see places that people are calling "home" that we wouldn't even keep an animal in. I don't think your pillow is going to be that important after tomorrow."

But by the end of the next day, she was no better. Haley continued to sob incessantly.

As the trip progressed, Haley's condition worsened.

I really didn't understand, and since I didn't have much patience left, I asked our Christian medical doctor to see her. He told me that she was fine physically, but she definitely had some emotional problems. He told me she was depressed.

I then got her to a Christian counselor who talked with her for hours. The counselor told me the same thing: "Haley's depressed."

Why hadn't it surfaced earlier? I don't know. I can only suspect that the stress of being in a foreign country—and away from her loved ones—caused some things to surface that she hadn't allowed herself to be aware of in the security of her tightly-knit family.

Haley spent the entire week and a half in tears. She was incapable of making any decisions at all. If I held up a Coke and a Pepsi and asked her which she wanted, she'd respond, "I don't know."

If I asked her if she wanted me to stick close to her the next day, she'd say, "I don't know."

When asked if she was ready for supper, you can guess what her response was, can't you? "I don't know."

It was as if she was turning into a vegetable. I was really confused . . . but Haley was depressed.

what is depression?

Before we talk about what depression is, let's first agree on what it's *not*. Amber catches up with you in the hall after school. You ask how it's going, and she responds: "We just had a pop quiz in science. I could have pulled an A if I'd known about it, but I probably made a C. I'm so depressed!"

Is Amber really depressed? No. She's bothered, but she's not actually in a state of depression.

Morgan calls you later: "I just heard that Heath is taking Erin to prom. You *know* how long I've had my eye on him. I am soooo depressed!"

Is Morgan truly depressed? No. She's bummed. She's sad. She may even be a little angry and jealous, but she's not actually in a state of depression.

We often use the term "depression" to describe a variety of feelings. Many times those feelings—sadness, grief, hopelessness, jealousy, anger, inferiority—can play a part of depression.

Nothing to laugh at, depression affects millions of people around the world—good people, Christians, actors, musicians, accountants, teachers, pastors . . . anyone can become depressed.

In order to help your friend through depression, it'll help first to understand a little about it. After all, there's more than one side to depression.

A Depressed Mood: This is usually linked directly to a specific situation and isn't long-term. For instance, if you've recently experienced a breakup with your boyfriend, you may feel deep sadness and grief for a few weeks, but eventually you'll get back to being yourself again.

Clinical Depression: When someone experiences this kind of depressions, it's more persistent and severe and isn't always linked to a specific cause such as a depressed mood mentioned above. Clinical depression has a variety of symptoms and can include these specific types of depression: *major depressive disorder, dysthymic disorder and bipolar disorder.*

I know. I know. Suddenly this is sounding like a medical dictionary instead of specific ways you can help a hurting friend. But stick with me, okay? I'll make it easy to understand. I promise. (Remember: you're reading this because you care about someone you think is depressed. So keep going.)

"There is a friend who STICKS CLOSER than a brother"
(Proverbs 18:24)

Here are some common symptoms that someone will experience if she has a major depressive disorder. But don't get scared if you've felt some of these things, too! Someone with a major depressive disorder will experience at least five of these symptoms for more than two weeks in such a way that it interferes with her daily life. (That's a big difference!)

- Irritable or sad most of the day—all day long.
- No longer interested in activities you once loved.
- Weight loss (without trying to lose) or weight gain (more than five percent of body weight in one month), loss of appetite or increased appetite.
- Not being able to sleep or sleeping too much nearly every day.
- Feeling tired and worn out nearly all day every day.
- Restlessness.
- Battling with huge amounts of guilt on a daily basis.
- Feeling of worthlessness—to the point of not being able to function in a positive demeanor.
- Lack of ability to concentrate or make decisions.

• Dwelling thoughts of death and/or suicide.

Dysthymic disorder: Teens with dysthymic disorder are usually cranky and hard to get along with as well as being depressed. They're usually very negative, critical and have a hard time relating to people their own age as well as adults.

Teens battling a dysthymic disorder usually have depressive symptoms for at least a year. Some of these symptoms are the same as one who's experiencing a major depressive disorder:
• Low energy, tired a lot
• Can't sleep—or sleeps too much
• Not hungry—or always hungry
• Lousy self-esteem
• Difficulty making decisions; hard to concentrate
• Feeling hopeless

Bipolar disorder: During the teen years, it's common—and even expected—to have fluctuating moods. But if you have a friend who's struggling with a bipolar disorder, her mood swings go beyond the normal teen changes. Her changes in mood will go from highly energetic—she'll talk constantly, have unending energy, not require much sleep, feel great about herself—or she'll be majorly depressed to the point of not being able to function normally.

now what?

Depression happens because of a variety of things—not because your friend is bad or crazy. Sometimes the chemicals in our brain just get a little off balance and we simply need to see a medical doctor who can prescribe medication to help realign those chemicals.

Sometimes depression is due to events that have happened in your friend's past, and she needs to see a counselor who can help pull out the buried hurt and show her how to deal with it. Other times, one will need medication *and* counseling to win the battle of depression.

A common mistake is to think that Christians should never get depressed because we have Jesus. Isn't that a little like saying Christians should never get the flu because we have Jesus? If our physical bodies wear out and become ill, why is it so hard to realize that our emotions, our mind and our brain sometimes need extra help as well?

A common mistake is to think that Christians should never get depressed because we have Jesus.

Of course, only a professional can truly diagnose depression, but here's a list of questions that may help you gain perspective on whether you or your friend may be experiencing depression. If you or your friend check yes to just one of these questions, you're experiencing sadness or anger. Everyone deals with that. But if your or your friend answer yes to *many*—and if you've experienced all of them close together (like in the past year), you'll probably battle with depression.

- ❑ Has there been a death in your family during the past year?
- ❑ Has a close friend died during the past year?
- ❑ Has your pet died or been lost in the past year?
- ❑ Have you recently broken up with your boyfriend?
- ❑ Do you have a close friend who has rejected or betrayed you in the past year?
- ❑ Has one of your best friends moved away in the past year?
- ❑ Have your folks separated or divorced in the past couple of years?
- ❑ Have your folks been fighting a lot more than usual during the past year?
- ❑ Do you see one of your parents a lot less than you used to?
- ❑ Has your family gone through a financial crisis in the past year? (Has Mom or Dad lost a job and is now unemployed?)
- ❑ Have you moved to a new location in the past year?
- ❑ Have you changed schools in the past year?
- ❑ Do you have a family member who has experienced serious depression in the past year?
- ❑ Has a brother or sister left home (college, marriage, job) in the past year?
- ❑ Does anyone in your family abuse alcohol or drugs?
- ❑ Do you have a family member who has been seriously injured in the past year?
- ❑ Have you experienced an injury or an illness in the past year that has forced you to cut back on normal activities?
- ❑ Do you have an on-going illness (epilepsy, diabetes) that limits your activity with friends or is a source of arguments between you and your folks?

- ❏ Have you been frequently concerned about recent body changes (starting your period, breast development, tall growth spurt, etc.)?
- ❏ Have you developed physically faster or slower than most of your friends, and do they tease you about it?
- ❏ Do you usually maintain a low self-esteem?
- ❏ Are you extremely critical of yourself?
- ❏ Do your folks place unreasonably high expectations on you and become upset when you don't meet those expectations?
- ❏ Do you have a family member who is very critical of you?
- ❏ Is it really tough to communicate right now with your folks? Are you yearning for a closeness that you used to enjoy with them?
- ❏ Do you have a learning disability?
- ❏ Is it hard for you to make or keep friends?
- ❏ Do you find yourself wondering obsessively if your parents really care about you?
- ❏ Are you feeling smothered by strict parents who don't allow you to express anger or share your opinions?
- ❏ Are you being emotionally or physically abused by someone close to you?
- ❏ Have you been sexually abused?
- ❏ Do other students gang up on you and give you a hard time?
- ❏ Do you feel like a failure when you do something that's less than your best—or when you make a grade that's not as high as you expected?
- ❏ Have you had a run-in with one of your teachers this past year?
- ❏ Has a stepparent been added to your family in the past year?
- ❏ Has your immediate family increased during the past year due to a birth, adoption, grandparent moving in, etc.?
- ❏ Do you have a brother or sister who has achieved so well in the past year that he/she has drawn your parents attention excessively to them? Have your folks often made remarks such as, "If you were more like (your bro/sis) . . ."

❏ Have you met a big goal recently (graduation, honors, special recognition) that has been exciting to you, but now that you've met it, you're feeling a letdown?

being a friend

DON'T:
- Say, "Snap out of it!" Someone who's depressed can't snap out of it. She needs help.
- Say, "I just don't get you any more. You're no fun."

DO:
- Say, "I don't really understand, but I'm here for you."
- Say, "Can we pray together regularly?"
- Give her lots of hugs.
- Write her encouraging notes
- Encourage her to talk with a professional (a pastor, a counselor, a doctor).
- Give her space when she needs it.
- Don't ignore her.
- Don't give up on her.

Sometimes we love our friends so much, it's hard for us to be objective when it comes to helping them. You may *want* to try to "force" your friend into getting help, but it really has to be her decision. Meanwhile, here are a few tips on what not to do and what can help.

How can you help your friend through depression? Well, you're not a counselor, you're a *friend*. So don't pretend to know all the answers or try to diagnose her. Love her like Jesus loves her. Be there for her. And again . . . encourage her to seek professional help.

helping a friend
who's
Trapped in the Internet

With the superinformation highway, we now have access to places and options we've never had before.

It still blows my mind to think that with a few simple clicks I can virtually be anywhere in the world. I recently went to the most primitive place in the world—Irian Jaya. Cannibals still live on this island and researchers remain in the process of counting and recording tribes.

It's accurate for me to say this place is at the end of the world. I had to take 20 flights in 12 days to get there and back. Once in Irian Jaya, I took a small plane and flew over rain forests and tropical jungle to a tiny village called Wahuka inhabited by the Kirikiri tribe.

These folks have never heard of electricity, refrigerators, bathtubs or bicycles. They're still living in the stone age, using pieces of rock attached by twine to sticks to accomplish their tasks.

Now, I'm not a big computer whiz. I'm really not. I know how to send e-mail, and I can surf the web (with a little help). But I'm in constant amazement that I can sit at my desk in Colorado Springs, turn on my computer and with a few clicks and entries find out what the exact temperature is on any given day in Wahuka! It's incredible! It's fantastic! But it's also frightening. With so much to access at our fingertips, we often overlook the danger of becoming too *involved* with the internet. It's easy to become "hooked" on chat rooms and communicating with people who can't see you.

You may have a friend who has fallen into this trap. Please take it seriously. The internet can be dangerous. And becoming obsessed with communicating with someone online can actually hamper your relationships with the friends you *can* see.

Check out this letter I received from a gal who's worried about her friend.

Dear Susie:

I have a friend who loves to visit chat rooms on her computer. She'll rush home from volleyball and go straight to her computer. Even when we're in youth group, she's constantly thinking about logging on when she gets home. I'm worried about her. Can't that be dangerous?

Frightened

Calgary, Alberta

I'm glad you're concerned about her. Yes, it can be dangerous—extremely dangerous—to be that involved in chat rooms. God wants us to live well-balanced lives and not be obsessive about anything.

Many teens, without even realizing it, have given out too much information online to strangers who later began stalking them or even worse.

When you're online, there's a false sense of security of being able to "talk" with someone who can't see you and who doesn't really know you. It feels safe to tell this person anything—what you're feeling, what you're struggling with and what your dreams for the future are.

The danger, though, comes in the fact that you have a clue who the other person is. He may tell you he's your age, that he goes to church and lives far away. But he may actually be twice your age, living in your same town and involved in pornography or other dangerous activities.

Please show the following story to your friend and try to convince her to not be so obsessive about getting online.

"Those who HOPE in the Lord will renew their strength. THEY WILL SOAR on wings like eagles; THEY WILL RUN and not grow weary, THEY WILL WALK and not be faint"

(Isaiah 40:31)

This Could Happen To You

If you ever go online, use e-mail or yak it up
in chat rooms, you've got to read this!
by Helen Walden & Sharon Sipos

Shannon could hear the footsteps behind her as she walked home. The thought of being followed made her heart beat faster. "You're being silly," she told herself. "No one's following you."

Just to be safe, she began to walk faster—but the footsteps kept up with her pace. Shannon said a quick prayer, "God, please keep me safe." She saw the porch light burning and ran the rest of the way to her house.

Once inside, she leaned against the door for a moment, relieved to be in the safety of her home. She glanced out the window to see if anyone was there. The sidewalk was empty.

After tossing her books on the sofa, Shannon decided to grab a snack and get online. There she could talk to strangers without being afraid. After all, no one knew who she really was, and no one could hurt her.

She logged on under her screen name, ByAngel213. Checking her Buddy List she saw GoTo123 was on. She sent him an instant message.

ByAngel213: Hi. I'm glad you're on! I thought someone was following me home today. It was really weird!

GoTo123: LOL You watch too much TV. Why would someone be following you? Don't you live in a safe neighborhood?

Shannon smiled at the computer code, LOL: *laugh out loud*.

ByAngel213: Of course I do . . . LOL . . . I guess it was my imagination . . . 'cause I didn't see anybody when I looked out.

GoTo123: Unless you gave your name online. . . . You haven't done that have you?

ByAngel213: Of course not. I'm not stupid, you know.

GoTo123: Did you have a softball game after school today?

ByAngel213: Yes, and we won!

GoTo123: What's your team called?

ByAngel213: We're the Canton Cats. We have tiger paws on our uniforms. They are really kewl.

GoTo123: Do you pitch or what?

ByAngel213: No. I play second base. I've got to go. My homework has to be done before my parents get home. I don't want them mad at me . . . Bye

GoTo123: Catch you later . . . Bye

Friend or Foe?

GoTo123 decided it was time to teach ByAngel213 a lesson—one she'd never forget. He went to the member menu and began to search for her profile. When it came up, he highlighted it and printed it out. He took out a pen and began to write down what he knew about Angel213 so far.

Her name: Shannon
Birthday: Jan 3, 1985
Age: 14
State where she lived: North Carolina
Hobbies: softball, chorus, skating and going to the mall

Along with this information, he knew she lived in Canton. She'd just told him that. He knew she stayed by herself until 6:30 every evening until her parents came home from work. He knew that she played softball on Thursday afternoons on the school team, the Canton Cats. Her favorite number, seven, was printed on her jersey. He knew she was in the eighth-grade at Canton Middle School.

Shannon gave all of this information to GoTo123 in the conversations they'd had online. He had enough information to find her now. *She'll be so surprised*, he thought. *She doesn't even know what she's done.*

The Search Is On

Shannon didn't tell her parents about the incident on the way home from the ballpark that day. She didn't want them to get hysterical and stop her from walking home from the softball games. Parents were always overreacting and her were the worst. It made her wish she was not an only child. Maybe if she'd had brothers and sisters her parents wouldn't be so overprotective.

By Thursday, Shannon had forgotten about the footsteps following her. Her game was in full swing when suddenly she felt someone staring at her. It was then that the memory came back.

She glanced up from her second base position to see a man watching her closely. He was leaning against the fence behind first base, and he smiled when she looked at him. He didn't look scary, so she quickly dismissed the fear she'd felt.

After the game, he sat on the bleachers while she talked to her coach. She noticed his smile once again as she walked past him. He nodded and she smiled back. He noticed her number on the back of the shirt. He knew he'd found her. Quietly, he walked a safe distance behind her. He didn't want to frighten her or have to explain to anyone what he was doing.

It was only a few blocks to Shannon's home and once he saw where she lived, he quickly returned to the park to get his car. Now he had to wait. He decided to get a bite to eat until the time came to go to Shannon's house. He drove to a fast food restaurant and sat there until it was time to make his move.

A Life-Saving Lesson

Shannon was in her room later that evening when she heard voices in the living room. "Shannon, come here," her father called. He sounded upset and she couldn't imagine why. She went into the room to see the man from the ballpark sitting on the sofa.

"Sit down," her father began. "This man is a retired policeman, and he's just told us a most interesting story about you."

Shannon moved cautiously to chair across from the man. *How could he tell her parents anything?* she thought. *I've never seen him before today!*

"Do you know who I am, Shannon?" the man asked.

"No," she answered.

"I'm your online friend, GoTo123."

Shannon was stunned. That's impossible! GoTo is a kid about my age! He's 15 and lives in Michigan!"

The man smiled. "I know I told you that, but it wasn't

true. You see, Shannon, there are people online who pretend to be kids; I was one of them.

"But while others do it to find kids and hurt them, I belong to a group of parents who do it to protect kids from predators. I came here tonight to let you know how dangerous it is to give out too much information to people online.

"You told me enough about yourself to make it easy for me to find you. Your name, the school you go to, the name of your ball team and the position you play. The number on your jersey just made finding you a breeze."

Shannon was stunned. "You mean you don't live in Michigan?"

He laughed. "No, I live in Raleigh. It made you feel safe to think I was so far away, didn't it?"

She nodded.

"I had a friend whose daughter was like you. Only she wasn't as lucky. The guy found her and murdered her while she was home alone. Kids are taught not to tell anyone when they are alone, yet they do it all the time online.

"The wrong people trick you into giving out information online—a little here and a little there. Before you know it, you've told them enough for them to find you without even realizing you've done it. I hope you've learned a lesson from this and won't do it again."

"I won't," Shannon promised.

"And will you tell others about this so they'll be safe, too?"

"It's a promise!"

That night Shannon told her parents about thinking someone had followed her home the week before. They listened as she assured them it had been her imagination, and she promised to tell them if anything like that happened again. Tears formed in her eyes as she recalled the prayer she'd prayed.

"You know," she said solemnly, "I asked God to keep me safe and He really has, hasn't He?"

How to Avoid Having This Happen to You

So, how much are you telling your online friends? Could someone find you if he or she wanted to? How much do you really know about the people you're talking with?

The story you just read isn't true. Yet it could have happened; it was based on true information given out to us by people online. It could easily happen to anyone who chats freely with strangers.

While it's not meant to frighten you, it is a lesson on how to be safe when you're online. This message is for guys as well as girls. Guys have been victims of online predators, too. So grab all your friends—guys and girls—and share the following way to protect yourself.

1. If you ever get aggressive, angry or abusive messages, tell your parents at once and contact the internet provider you use to seek assistance.

2. Some of you probably won't like this, but we strongly suggest that you avoid chat rooms altogether. Experts agree that chat rooms are by far the most dangerous Internet activity, for the reasons that were shown through our story.

3. Never tell anyone your full name, address, phone number, city or any other personal information about yourself or your family.

4. If you use America Online or CompuServe, watch what information you include on your profile. Don't put your date of birth, especially the year. If you use Netscape, Explorer or Mosaic to connect through a local service provider, don't enter your full name—especially your last name—when you configure the software for e-mail and news groups. This also applies if you use a separate program to get your e-mail. Many people know how to get your street address armed with nothing but your last name and the name of your service provider. Remember—you don't have to give out any information you don't want to.

5. If you still choose to be in a chat room or are using e-mail and someone asks you personal questions, such as where you go to school, where you live or any other personal questions you don't feel comfortable answering, don't hesitate to write, "I'm sorry, I don't give out personal information" or "My parents have asked me not to tell that."

6. If someone sends you an e-mail form with personal information about himself or herself on it and suggests you fill one out just like it, be alerted and don't do it. You have no idea to whom or where it will be forwarded!

7. If, once again, you decide to be in a chat room and anyone pressures you to talk, won't leave you alone or asks for personal information, get offline immediately.

8. Don't respond to e-mail from people you don't know. If you believe you've received something strange, tell your parents.

9. Never agree to meet anyone whom you've met online face-to-face.

Most importantly: **Has any of this already happened to you?** If it has, this is a great time to tell your parents. You may also write us with any questions or suggestions at: **TeenFocus@aol.com** or **TeenFocus1@aol.com**

Who Are We?

We are two mature, dedicated Christians who have a real concern for the safety of young people online. We've recently witnessed several instances where young people have given out or been asked to give out all kinds of personal information.

The people asking for this information were strangers. Because of this, we've formed a group called Teen Focus. We hope to send out a newsletter on a regular basis with fun and safe things teens can participate in on the Web.

In the world of the internet, people can say they are anyone they want and none of us have any way of knowing who they really are. We want to help you. Please show this article to your parents and pass it along to any friends you think may benefit form it.

For more information on this subject, check out Focus on the Family's CitizenLink Internet resource page on the Web at: **www.family.org/cforum/hotissues/A0001919.html**

The above article by Helen Walden and Sharon Sipos appeared in the January 1999 issue of Brio magazine.

what can you do?

Again, I'm glad you're concerned about your friend. You have reason to be. I'm also proud of you for wanting to help her. First, show her the above story, then get together and talk about it. Ask her how she felt after she read the story. Point out that serious crimes are being committed daily by folks taking advantage of teenagers through the Internet.

Next, ask her if you can hold her accountable to do the following:

- Begin gradually limiting her involvement on the Internet. For example, suggest that she not even turn her computer on for two days this week. Hold her accountable. On those two days, get together and pray with her. Next week she gives up chat rooms, etc. Again, pray together as she releases this involvement to God. She's giving something up that she's enjoying, so she may be angry, sad, frustrated. And she may take some of those emotions out on you. That's okay. Be prepared. Continue to pray with her.
- Help her find other activities to replace her time spent on the Internet. Start a Bible study together. Learn a new hobby. Look for a part-time job together. Take a pottery class.
- Continue to stick close to her even after she's given up her involvement on the Internet. Keep holding her accountable in a gentle way. Ask her to let you know when she's tempted to fall back into a chat room. That temptation will probably hit her when she's feeling lonely or sad. Be there for her.

Computers are incredible machines. Make it your goal to help your friend find *balance*. In other words, don't expect her to never turn on her computer again. There are so many advan-

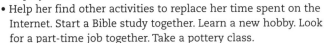

"He who covers over an offense PROMOTES LOVE, but whoever repeats the matter separates close friends"
(Proverbs 17:9)

tages to having the superinformation highway and access that we have. She'll need that information for school and research. The key, though, is balance. Encourage her to continue using the computer to enhance her knowledge and improve her school work, but to steer away from chat rooms and online relationships.

how to Help your hurting friend

helping a friend
Cope with
an Illness

Brooke and Keisha had been friends for three years when Keisha was diagnosed with diabetes. "She started pulling away from me," Brooke says. "Keisha became kind of angry and distant. I want her know that we're still best friends. Okay, so she's got diabetes. Our friendship shouldn't have to suffer. I care about Keisha, and I want to help her through this time of adjustment."

Maybe you, like Brooke, have a friend who's trying to cope with an illness or disease. The key word that Brooke used is "adjustment." As your friend learns how to adjust her lifestyle to necessary changes, you may need to give a little more in order to help her adjustment go more smoothly.

For example, Keisha now has to eat a balanced diet on a very regular schedule. She also has to test her blood sugar level and give herself insulin injections. She'll need some space at first. Allow her time to get used this—she's going through some major changes.

A friend who has epilepsy may not be able to get her driver's license. Realize, as you reach out to your friend, that she's dealing with some major disappointment. How would you feel if you'd had your heart set on driving and recently found out you'd have to give up that dream?

It's also tough on your friend with special needs to realize she doesn't always fit in. Maybe she can't swim because she's confined to a wheelchair. Or perhaps she can't participate in team sports due to her blindness. Whatever the illness or disease, your friend probably feels isolated a lot and goes through more hurt than she's letting on.

You can be an encouragement to her. *You* can help her realize that God can use every illness, each setback, every handicap to bring glory to Him.

I met 17-year-old Nann when she stopped by my office at *Brio* magazine. As she began telling our staff about herself, we decided to turn on the tape recorder so we could share her story with others. Check it out.

Here I Am!
Saying it's what's on the inside that counts is one thing–believing it and living it are another.
by Marty McCormack

"Ugh! I'm having such a *bad* hair day!"

Remember mumbling these words under your breath as you headed to school last week—and the countless times you repeated them as you stood in front of the bathroom mirror with your friends, desperately doing whatever you could to remedy the horrible situation surrounding your head?

Most of us have had days when we've been less than thrilled with our uncooperative hair. *Some* of us have gone so far as to consider chopping it all off. But not *all* of us.

Eighteen-year-old Nann Chafin is one girl who's not complaining about her hair. That's because since she was 12, Nann hasn't had much hair to complain about. Within a few months of her hairstylist first discovering a dime-sized bald spot on the back of her head, Nann went from a full head of thick, blond curls to a head with a few strands of hair here and there.

Upon noticing the initial bald spot in August 1993, Nann's hairstylist said it looked like *alopecia areata,* an auto-immune deficiency, and suggested that she visit a dermatologist. Nann's mom called a doctor from the salon, and after a consultation the dermatologist confirmed that Nann had *alopecia areata.*

The Scoop on Alopecia

So what does it mean to have an auto-immune deficiency that makes your hair fall out? Simply, it means that

Nann's immune system thinks she's allergic to her own hair. There are different varieties of *alopecia*. Nann has *totalis*—it affects only her head. People who have *universalis alopecia* lose all their hair—eyebrows, eyelashes, leg hair, etc. Others who have less severe cases resulting in a patch of missing head hair or arm hair may not even realize they have *alopecia*. Because *alopecia* is so rare, and because it is not life-threatening, the government hasn't allocated much money to research the condition. No one knows how or why a person may have it. And without much research, there haven't been any great strides made in finding a helpful treatment or cure.

Though Nann says she wasn't worried about the first bald spot even when it grew to the size of a silver dollar, her dermatologist must have been. She immediately gave Nann more than 30 different medications to take at the same time.

"I became really weak from all the steroids, and I blew up like a balloon," Nann says.

Even though she's no longer taking all the medication, Nann still has a lot of pain in her joints. She expects she'll have some type of arthritis for the rest of her life.

More Than a Bad Hair Day

By January 1994, Nann's head was covered with bald spots. As her hair began to thin, she accumulated a collection of hats and got permission to wear them to her public school.

"For a long time I had a little bit of hair on the side of my head," Nann explains. "I could tease that and curl it and make it look like I had a little bit more hair than I did.

"I wore hats, but kids can be cruel. I remember this guy came up and jerked my hat off. People were standing around, and then all of a sudden they just stopped and stared. It was like they didn't know if they should do something, or if they should laugh. Some *did* laugh.

"I said to this guy, 'Are you finished?' He snickered and tried to be cool. So I said, 'Can I have my hat back, please?' He reluctantly returned it, and I put it back on. I said goodbye and walked down the stairs.

"It was the end of the school day, and I went home and told my mom, 'I'm not going back.' She woke me up the next morning for school, and I said, 'Mom, I'm not going back.' She said, 'Okay, we'll get the necessary papers to school you at home.'"

In Search of One True Friend

Before Nann opted for home schooling, she was involved with several activities at her school. Even while she was dealing with the effects of *alopecia* and the medications she was taking, she didn't let her pain keep her from making worthwhile contributions.

When Nann realized there wasn't a student choir at her school, she recruited an interested teacher and students and went before the school board and principal to request a choir. Today the school has a chorus program and Nann is invited to come back for concerts.

Nann says students thought a lot of her—when she had a full head of hair. Instead of having just *one* group of friends, she was in *every* group. During lunch she'd often move from table to table to visit with as many people as possible.

But once she started losing her hair, Nann began losing "friends" too.

"I used to have a seat saved for me all the time at lunch," she remembers. "Once I started losing my hair and wearing hats to school, I'd walk up and there'd be no seats.

"When I'd sit down, people would literally get up and move. Even when we'd be walking somewhere, everyone would get in this huddle with the backs to me and leave me completely out.

"I basically had the same people in all my classes, and they didn't talk to me anymore. Whenever I'd put my fingers through my hair or put it behind my shoulder to lean down, I'd have to shake hair off. People complained about getting hair on their desk. When something like this happens, you really find out who your true friends are."

As if classes and lunch time being unbearable wasn't enough, Nann had to deal with insensitivity from teens during other parts of the school day as well.

"Girls would go into the bathroom after lunch to brush their hair and freshen up for the rest of the day. When I did that, it was just embarrassing," she says.

"I wouldn't try to brush my hair, but I'd wait for other girls to do theirs. They'd said, 'Oh, I *hate* my hair! It never does anything right. I'd stand there thinking, *If you only knew. . . .*"

Looking for the Bright Side

When Nann finally decided she'd had enough of public school, her dermatologist reluctantly signed her homebound papers. She hesitated because she thought Nann needed to get on with her life and be out in public. To Nann's dermatologist, dealing with *alopecia* seemed like no big deal. She didn't understand the middle-school world Nann was living in that put so much importance on a person's outer appearance.

Once Nann was away from daily contact with other teens, she realized just how much she depended on God. "I know God helped me through everything," she says.

"It's been hard to explain because it's so personal—between God and me. I finally figured out that He helped me one day at a time. Sometimes for an hour at a time. He helped me little by little.

"I never, *never* let go of God. I never doubted Him. But sometimes I'd get frustrated. Sometimes I'd think, *I know what I don't have. . . . I don't have my hair, I don't have my friends at school, I don't even have school anymore.*"

"One day, I decided to sit down and think of what I *did* have. I thought and I thought. Finally I just said, "I've got God. That's what I've got. I've got God, and my youth group, and my family.'

"What in the world would I do if I let go of God? What would I have? I'd have just this negative, nothing. I'd probably be in a fetal position on the floor somewhere, all depressed. Thank God that He didn't let *me* let go of *Him*."

While Nann is highly involved in her youth group, she says she still goes for days without getting one phone call from a friend. Sometimes she thinks friends in her church don't realize that they're even more valuable to her now since she doesn't have connections with teens at school anymore.

"I'd love to have friends call and tell me what happened at school, or have them ask about my day at home school," she says. "Sometimes the support just isn't there. It still comes down to one or two. God, and one or two people."

Firm Foundation

Once during a service at church, Nann went to the altar for prayer. "I told my pastor, 'I want you to pray for my *alopecia*.' He started praying for me, but the entire prayer was for my 'Aunt Patricia.' I was laughing, and he thought I was crying and was patting my back."

Along with prayer, whether for her *alopecia* or non-existent Aunt Patricia, Nann has gained much of her strength through Scripture. Paraphrasing Psalm 46, Nann says, "I love how it says, Nations will rise up against you and mountains

'Girls would go into the bathroom after lunch to brush their hair and freshen up for the rest of the day. when I did that, it was just embarrassing'

will crumble, and all of a sudden He says, 'Be still, and know that I am God.' When it gets to that part, peace comes over me. Just be still, and know that I am God, and I am here. That's all I need to know.

"I just read somewhere that faith is neither sight, nor sense, nor reason, but just simply believing in God. Just believe in God. Faith the size of a mustard seed can move mountains, so if just believing in God can move mountains, think what can happen if you believe that God can perform miracles!"

She's Back!

Before Nann left South Carolina to visit the *Brio* staff in Colorado, she said something to her youth pastor that blew him away. "When I come back," she said, "I might stop wearing my wig."

When Nann showed up in *Brio* land, she was without the wig, but wore a purple scarf wrapped around her head. It matched her sweater perfectly. A few weeks after we met Nann, her mom wrote to fill us in on how Nann was doing. Here's an excerpt from her letter.

"I must give you this update on Nann. Her interview has inspired and strengthened her. When we returned home, she found the courage to go before her youth group and share a little of what she's been through. She then told of her desire to not wear her wig anymore around them. Many of them didn't even know she wore a wig.

"With tears streaming down her face, Nann said, 'I'm not wearing my wig anymore, and I need to know it's all right with all of you.' Sobbing, she reached up and slowly, deliberately, took off her hair in front of more than 50 teens and adults.

"That night, with the strength from God through the encouragement of her interview with *Brio*, Nann was free from bondage—after five years we feel our Nann is back. She's bruised and broken, but brave, strong and once again flashing that huge smile with freedom behind it.

"Sometimes God chooses not to physically heal, but He always heals in His own way and chooses our paths for His glory!"

If you'd like more information about *alopecia areata,* write to the National Alopecia Areata Foundation at P.O. Box 150760, San Rafael, CA 94915-0760.

knowledge from nann

With all that Nann's experienced in going from a sought-after beauty pageant contestant to a teen without hair, you'd expect that she's learned something about life. Well, she has. Here are some thoughts she has to share with you.

Acceptance:

"I've learned that people can accept somebody in a wheel-chair, or somebody without an arm, but when I come in without hair, it's like 'Oh, she looks sooo sick. What's wrong with her? Better not get too close.'

"Some people let go of their friendship with me. I think that they finally got too frustrated trying to understand what was going on in my life. They didn't just accept it.

"When you meet someone who's going through a battle, just accept it and be a friend. I'd much rather have people come up to me and say, 'How'd you lose your hair,' than just stare or give me funny looks."

Beauty:

"The things of this world absolutely do not matter. I've been in beauty pageants. In fact, the Miss America Pageant contacted me many times asking me to represent South Carolina. I never responded.

"We put so much focus on appearances. I've won first place in talent competitions and was so active in school, but when it comes right down to where the rubber hits the road, all that matters is faith in God."

Challenges:

"For those who have any kind of a challenge—physical or emotional—try not to get mad at God and ask, 'Why me? Why did this happen to me?' You need to know God is not trying to punish you because you're not good enough. He thinks you *are* good enough. You are good enough for Him to be able to place a challenge before you, knowing that you can handle it and take it like a woman!

"Have your week of grieving over it, because you need that grieving and closure. Then go out there and say, 'Okay, I'm finished with all the crying. God, what do You want me to do with this? Show me how You want me to use this.' The hard times are going to come, and they're going to be awful, but God can help you through it if you have that kind of an attitude.

With tears streaming down her face, Nann said, 'I'm not wearing my wig anymore, and I need to know it's all right with all of you.'

"God has placed every situation and every detail of everything that you go through there for a reason. One day He'll place something in your life, and you'll think, *This is why God has given me this.* And it will be worth every bit of the struggle.

"For me, that time is when I give my testimony and people come up to me and say, 'God sent you here just for me.' The first time I gave my testimony, a lady leaned over behind me and said in my ear, 'I've been contemplating suicide, and you changed my mind completely.'

"Of course, that was God through me, but when she said that, I was thinking, *It's worth everything then, I've saved a life! God saved a life through me.*"

update on nann

Since meeting Nann two years ago, a lot of exciting things have happened in her life! She has received numerous invitations for speaking engagements and enjoys sharing her testimony wherever God opens a door.

Nann's going without her wig every day now. Well, almost every day—she *does* put it on occasionally for fun. Nann completed her senior year of high school at a local Christian school and graduated with 60 in her class.

Even though she has had many exciting opportunities in the past couple of years, she's experienced some difficult times, too. A few months ago, she spent time in the hospital battling mono-hepatitis with pneumonia. Nann is currently attending college and enjoying making new friends.

I'm excited that Nann is able to maintain such a positive attitude while struggling with a disease that affects her personal appearance. The key, of course, is her personal relationship with Christ. God is faithful to bring Christians into our lives who can encourage us and strengthen our walk with Him when we juggle doubts and confusion due to illness or disease.

You can be Jesus to your friend with an illness. Here are a few things that might help.

DON'T:
- Say, "Children are starving overseas, and you're worried about your illness?"
- Say, "It must be God's will."
- Ignore her pain or illness. Acting like it doesn't exist won't make it go away or help her feel any better.
- Bring special attention to her pain or illness.

DO:
- Take your cues from her. If she has arthritis and needs to rest a while before you continue shopping at the mall, sit with her.
- Understand that she has limitations. Accept them.
- Genuinely affirm her. Does her hair look especially nice today? Tell her. She aced the English test? Brag on her. She's especially good with children? Point that out to her.
- Laugh a lot together.

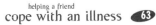

Meet another young lady whose strong relationship with Christ gives her the strength needed to juggle a terminal illness.

Blessing In Disguise
by Becky Clemmons

In 1982, at the age of 5 months, doctors told my parents I wouldn't live to see my first birthday. I was diagnosed with the fatal disease cystic fibrosis (CF). I did live to celebrate my first birthday, however, as well as my second and third and fourth—actually I've seen 16 birthdays come and go.

I was hospitalized 17 times before I turned 14, and I've been in 13 more times since then. Most of these hospitalizations have been three to four weeks at a time. That means for a good part of my life, I've spent about every other month in the hospital. I do chest physiotherapy and nebulized breathing treatments twice daily, take 30 pills a day and get additional medicines intravenously every weekend. During the week I receive therapy at BroMenn hospital in my hometown everyday; and then on weekends I do more at home.

I make the four-hour trip to the doctor in Iowa City often and still have to keep up my schoolwork in order to graduate in two more years. My freshman year I missed about three-fourths of the school year due to hospitalizations. I had to continue to do schoolwork into the summer so I wouldn't have to repeat that year.

I've had to grow up very quickly in my 16 years and have had to face the fact that the average life expectancy for a child with CF is only 30 years. I know that CF is the No. 1 genetic killer of children and young adults in the United States. I've had to watch many of my teenage friends with CF die— some who have appeared to be healthier than me. I've had to understand that the next time it could be me.

Life With God

I'd like to tell you that this was my life *before* God . . . but I can't. This is my life *with* God. You hear stories of tragedies and then hear at the end of the stories that the people found God and their lives completely turned around with no more worries or troubles—and this is wonderful. It's healing to hear people's stories and think that others just need to find God and everything will be wonderful. Unfortunately, I am not one of those people.

I grew up in a Christian home knowing that an early death could be my fate. I could have chosen to let myself go and feel sorry for myself. But someone told me that God had something more than just a life with an illness planned for me. I believe with all my heart that I was given this disease for a purpose. I believe I was given this so I could tell all of you that even with a disease like the one I have, I still have a wonderful life with God and I am still an optimist. I have seen a lot of non-Christian psychiatrists who can't believe that a person my age with this disease can be so positive. They think that I'm only denying the inevitable.

But they don't know why I can be this positive. They don't know the Great Physician. They don't understand why I'm not afraid of death, even though I know I could die at any time, because they don't know the loving and powerful God I do. They don't realize that the reason I'm always smiling is because the joy of the Lord truly is my strength.

The Best If Yet to Come

Doctors haven't found a cure for CF yet, and my insurance company hasn't been too glad to pay my bills, but I still have hope. I hope that doctors will find a cure, but I also know that no matter what, a time will come when I won't have to deal with any of this anymore.

Heaven is a wonderful place where there are no more troubles, no more worries, no more heartaches and no more diseases. I look forward to the day when I can see the Great Physician's face and thank Him for giving me this.

I have helped people to know that there really is a God who loves everybody. He didn't give me this disease because He wanted to hurt me. Instead, I believe He allowed me to have this gift so I could touch other's lives—like yours—and let you know that no matter what, Someone is always there for you. And Someone is always there to listen when you have problems, joys and tears.

Again, try to help your friend realize that God can use her testimony about her illness to help others who are struggling. Encourage her to talk openly about how she feels physically and emotionally. If she agrees, help her jot down some of the things she's learning through her illness. Ask her to practice giving her testimony in front of you. In time, ask her if you can suggest to your youth pastor that she share with your youth group.

You've probably read, seen or heard the testimony of Joni Earekson Tada. She was paralyzed in a diving accident during her teen years and is confined to a wheelchair. She writes and paints by holding a pen or brush in her mouth. She's authored several books, has her own national ministry, "Joni and Friends," and has even released a movie based on her story.

I'm so glad Joni allowed God to use her disappointment to encourage others.

And I'll never forget meeting Gianna Jessen. As an unwanted pregnancy, Gianna was aborted—but survived! During her teen years, she began sharing her testimony around the nation. She is refusing to allow her scars to hold her down.

And then there's 17-year-old Amy Graham who was born with no thumbs. First grade was terrible for her. Kids would say things like, "Eeew, don't touch me. You don't have thumbs" and "Give me five—oh wait, you can't." Amy learned early on what being made fun of was all about.

But she kept a positive attitude. Sometimes when kids first noticed that she didn't have thumbs she'd respond with, "Oh, I left them at home in my drawer," or she'd act incredibly surprised and say, "Oh, my! I don't have thumbs!"

When Amy reached junior high, it became harder to deal with painful comments. "My seventh-grade science teacher pointed me out during class one time when he was talking about deformities. He said, 'Yeah, like Amy. Amy's deformed and abnormal.' "

When she entered high school, she decided to deepen her relationship with Christ. "I was a Christian in junior high, but since I wasn't spending time with God like I should have been, I always felt like I was missing something," she says. "I finally realized that nothing could fill my life—drugs, alcohol, friends, being popular, looking good—except God."

Amy has also battled feelings of inferiority toward her sister. "She's absolutely gorgeous!" she says. "I always felt inferior to her because she's older and really beautiful, *and she has thumbs!* It took me awhile to realize that God has made me a special person, too.

"God continues to teach me that our inner beauty is *so much*

But someone told me that God had something more than just a life with an illness planned for me.

more important than our outer beauty. Everything on our outside can fade away; we grow older, we get wrinkly, we're not always young and youthful-looking.

"But inside we either grow stronger or we fall away. Staying close to God is so much more important than chasing outer beauty because that relationship is what's going to stay with you always."

ministry-minded amy

As Amy has accepted herself for who God created her to be, she has also come to count her uniqueness as a blessing. "Not having thumbs has brought so many opportunities for me to witness to people about my faith in God," she says.

Throughout her 17 years of life, Amy has discovered there aren't many things she can't do. She's active in band, sports, serves on the youth council at her church and is president of Fellowship of Christian Athletes at her school.

What *can't* she do? Well, hitchhike, give a thumbs-up sign and do conventional sign language.

In tough times Amy has clung to her faith, her family and the Bible.

Psalm 139 reveals that God has created Amy, Gianna, Becky and Nann's inmost being and knit them personally in their mother's womb. Each one is fearfully and wonderfully made—even with limitations.

What God will do with a willing heart is beyond our wildest dreams. It doesn't matter to Him if that willing heart is inside a weak body; He's simply looking for obedient disciples.

"Pleasant words are a honeycomb, SWEET TO THE SOUL and healing to the bones"
(Proverbs 16:24)

how to Help your hurting friend

helping a friend
through Self-
Destruction

Imagine holding so much hurt on the inside that experiencing great physical pain on the outside would seem minor.

Chava was 15 years old when she started hurting herself. "I had a really low self-esteem," she says, "and I was always condemning myself." In an effort to take her mind off of the deep hurt she was harboring in her heart, Chava began cutting herself and burning her arms with a curling iron.

If you have a friend who is experiencing with self-mutilation, he or she may be known as a "cutter." It's dangerous, and your friend may be stuck with physical scars for a lifetime.

It's difficult to understand why someone would voluntarily inflict pain on herself, isn't it? No one simply begins cutting herself for the fun of it. It's painful. Someone who is involved in self-destructive habits is a friend who is hurting reallyreallyreally bad! Oftentimes, they're trying to cover up a painful experience from the past or are trying to call out for help.

What can you do to help? First, let me share a little more of Chava's story to help you better understand what your friend may be feeling.

Chava's pain happened right before she entered her teen years. "When I was 11," she says, "my family moved to Israel. While on vacation at a beach, I was raped by a 29-year-old lifeguard."

She didn't tell anyone, because since he offered her a ride, and she voluntarily got in the car with him, she assumed the rape was her fault. And she was embarrassed.

"I didn't know what to do with all that hurt," she continues. "It just wouldn't go away. It kept growing and knawing at my insides."

Despite the nightmare she experienced at the beach, Chava enjoyed living in another country and learning about a different culture. "My dad is a rabbi," she says, "and my family loved being in Israel."

But when she turned 15, her dad decided to move the family back to the United States. "I didn't want to come back," Chava explains. "I became very bitter about having to move again—and having to move such a long distance. I was just getting used to the culture, the food, the climate and the people."

trying to fit in

When Chava arrived back in the States, she felt like an outsider. "I spent a lot of time trying to figure out where I fit in," she remembers. "All my friends had changed. It was really hard to find common ground with anyone—even with my best friends. They all thought I was weird."

> "My command is this: LOVE EACH OTHER as I have loved you."
> (John 15:12)

Chava discovered one of her friend's was bulimic. "I had always carried a phobia about my weight," she says, "and the fact that my one friend was bulimic influenced me to obsess about my own weight."

Because Chava was still hiding the pain from being raped, it didn't take long for her to attempt to fill the void in her life by controlling her weight. She began throwing up three times a day and finally got to the point where eating anything made her physically sick.

Her parents noticed the changes in their daughter and tried to help, but because Chava was determined to continue hiding her pain, they were limited in what they could do. They *did*, however, get her into counseling.

the hurt won't go away

Not only was she dealing with the secret of being raped, weight fluctuation and rejection from friends, Chava's grandpa shot himself and died a month after she had returned from Israel. "I saw him one day, and he died the next," she remembers.

"I didn't want to keep thinking about all the hurt inside me. I was desperate to get my mind off all the sadness and confusion I was feeling," she says. So one day at a friend's house, when Chava was 15, she took a sewing needle and scraped her hands and arms. "Later, I told my mom that my friend's cat had scratched me," she says.

"Part of me was thinking, *I can't believe I'm doing this.* But the other part of me was someone able to numb the pain on the *inside* because now I was focusing on a different pain—a physical pain on the *outside.*"

is there hope?

Chava was finally hospitalized because of excessive cutting and because of a suicide attempt. She was diagnosed with major depression and was placed in a locked down facility. "I felt very far from God," she remembers. "I kept thinking, *He won't love me. Why would He? I'm too unworthy. I'm worth nothing.*

But Chava's parents and church family continued to love her and pray for her. When she was released from the hospital, she began attending a weekly women's Bible study with her mom. "It was four hours long," she says. "We'd bring our workbooks and read out loud and really dig into the Scripture."

Chava had loved dancing since she was a child, and one day the Bible study group was listening to some soft music during their prayer and worship time. "The song was El Shadai," Chava remembers. "I've always loved that song. I felt God was touching me in a special way. During the next few minutes, I got up and danced the song for the women."

Afterward, the women surrounded Chava and prayed with her. "I gave God 100 percent," she says. "I gave Him everything! I can't go back to the hospital. I can't continue to self-destruct. I can't keep destroying the temple God has given me."

Is she still tempted? "I'll be honest," Chava says. "I still struggle with the temptation to cut myself. I'm still battling bulimia, but God is working with me. Some of my healing may take time,

'...part of me was someone able to numb the pain on the inside because now I was focusing on a different pain—a physical pain on the outside.'

but He's not giving up on me. I've surrendered myself to His care, and with His help, I know I'll make it.

"Strengthen the feeble hands, STEADY THE KNEES that give way; say to those with fearful hearts, 'Be strong, do not fear; YOUR GOD WILL COME'"
(Isaiah 35:3-4)

"I'm so much closer now to my parents," Chava says. "The biggest help they've given me is to make me realize they're not giving up on me. They hug me a lot.

They smile with their eyes as well as their mouth, and they show me in a million ways that they love me.

"My parents bought me a journal and assured me that it was for all my private thoughts and that no one would ever read it unless I chose to share it. There's such a security in that. So, I'm writing down my thoughts now," she says. "That really clears my head. I love to write poetry.

"Later, I go back and re-read what I've written and it helps me gain a clearer perspective of what I'm struggling with. I also try to listen to calming music. Some of my favorites are: Twila Paris, Kim Hill, Nicole Nordeman and Point of Grace."

DON'T:
- Condemn her. Your friend already knows what she's doing isn't right.
- Point attention to the physical scars. She knows they're disgusting. Remember those scars have come out of great pain. Your friend doesn't know how to accept herself. She hates who she is.

DO:

- Watch for warning signs: Wearing long shirts when it's not cold (to cover scars from cutting or burning), overly modest (not wanting to change in front of people), wearing shorts and a shirt over a swim suit (so no one will see the scars).
- Ask your friend straight-out if she's cutting or burning herself.
- Give your friend lots of hugs.
- Encourage her to get professional help. Check with your pastor for a list of Christian counselors to recommend. Remember, it's not simply a few cuts or burns. Your friend is trying to cover up something much worse.

What can you do to help your friend who may be in a similar situation?

Ask your friend if the two of you can get together at least once a week to read the Bible together. Ask God to speak words of love and affirmation to her through your reading.

Also, encourage her to journal, like Chava is doing, or to release their pent-up anger through physical activity like jogging, slamming tennis balls against a backboard, biking or hitting a punching bag. Even though a punching bag will cost a few dollars, it'll be worth every penny spent to keep from hurting herself.

Remember those scars have come out of great pain. Your friend doesn't know how to accept herself. She hates who she is.

helping a friend
who has been
Sexually
Abused

There are many types of sexual abuse: incest, rape, molestation, date rape. Because most of my experience in helping teens through sexual abuse has been in the area of incest, much of this chapter will focus on that.

Much of what you'll read in the next few pages, however, will apply to someone who has experienced *any* kind of sexual abuse.

Let's begin with a page from my journal during my days as a youth minister:

Sharing the Pain
I took 48 high school teenagers on tour.
After our successful evening performance
they were too excited to call it a night.

Their spontaneity turned the hotel parking
lot into a Broadway stage. Creative energy
personified itself in the midnight Houston
humidity. Rhythm from portable stereos
became live motion.

Nearby, gymnastics into the deep end of the
midsize pool exploded like fireworks.

I expected your laughter and talent to perme-
ate the after-hours celebration. Instead, you sat
alone . . . tears glistening against the moonlight.

I strained to distinguish your soft words

against the electrified tones just meters away.

Like bread torn in communion, you broke each
word and gave it away in desperation.

**"Things at home.
It's my dad.
He . . ."**

My energy turned to anger. Fireworks **burned** inside my soul.
I enforced a curfew. The music stopped.
Completely.

The parking lot empty, I returned to you—
a 16-year-old child-adult sitting alone on the curb
outside the Holiday Inn in Houston, Texas.

I was naive. Didn't know *anything* about incest.
But I *did* know the Shepherd always headed for
the hurting sheep. So I held you in my arms and
rocked you . . . as if motion could somehow
comfort the pain.
We cried for two and a half hours.

The remainder of the tour brought great reviews.
But the rhythm was never the same.
The music died with Emily—the 16-year-old child-adult.

"Whatever is TRUE, whatever is NOBLE,
whatever is RIGHT, whatever is PURE,
whatever is LOVELY, whatever is ADMIRABLE-
if anything is excellent or PRAISEWORTHY-
THINK about such things"
(Philippians 4:8)

That's how *I* felt as her youth minister and her friend. To
understand what *she* felt—or what your friend may be feeling—
keep reading as we both share thoughts and feelings from our
journals. I'll put Emily's entries in a different font, so you can
easily tell us apart.

They tell us quite often how to protect ourselves
when on the street or when out after dark . . .

But why doesn't anyone tell us how to protect
ourselves after dark in our own homes?

And sometimes even when all the lights are still on?

Today instead of doing our times threes
the teacher said we would have a special lesson.

It was about safety and stuff.
She told us what to do
if anyone abused our bodies.

"Tell your parents," the teacher said.

So I told Mommy. She yelled and said I was bad.
Then she sent me to bed without any supper.

Why did I tell?

Now, tonight when he comes home,
it will hurt worse than ever . . .

I'm so scared.
And Teacher . . .you were wrong.

It was the middle of September.
Dad came home early.
The school bus had barely dropped me off
and I had invited Rachel over to play hopscotch.
Dad told me to come inside . . .
said he had come home early just to be with me.

My stomach tensed.
My legs began to shake.
I begged to finish playing hopscotch with Rachel.
We had just started.
Dad sent her home.
When I still refused, he grabbed my arm
and jerked my whole body off the ground and into the house.

It hurt.
I screamed.
Rachel ran.

Dad was so strong.
I was so small.
and frightened.
He always got his way.

. . . and Rachel never came back.

It's happening again.
The lights are out and
Mommy sent me to bed hours ago.
She told me to sleep tight
so I would remember how to write all the words
on the spelling test tomorrow.

But I can't go to sleep.
I'm scared.
My face is all wet and sticky from tears.
Your rough hands are hurting me.

I will hold my teddy bear a little closer.
clutch him a little tighter
. . . and once again
pretend I am at Amy's house
and we are having tea
with her new dishes.

It wasn't until the eighth grade
that I realized what was going on
between us was not normal.

I had always hated it.
And it always made me physically sick.
But you said every family was like this.
And because "parents are always right,"
I believed you.

Then came Friday.
Traci and I spent the night at her house
so we could work on our book reports together.

My report was on journalism.
Hers was on something called incest.

I've never heard of it before.

She let me thumb through the book.
So that's what they call it.
I didn't even know there was a name
for what you had forced me to do.

I asked Traci if it was wrong.
She said it was.
Said people could go to jail for it.
I gave the book back.
afraid to read the words
for fear of my name being
somewhere on the pages.

Then I ran into the bathroom and threw up.

....

Today in biology class
we saw the sex education films
and had open discussion afterward.

All the other kids listened intently
interrupting only occasionally
with nervous giggles.

I tried to pretend
that I was as interested as everyone else.
But the subject was not new to me.
My firsthand experience
went a lot further
than the chapter we were studying.

I got physically ill
and was sent to the nurse's office.
She said it was probably the flu.
I knew better.

What would it feel like, I wondered,
to simply be a student . . . and not a victim?

....

Just once
I'd like to be hugged by you
the way Bethany's dad hugs her.
Just once
I'd like to sit next to you
and not have to worry about your hands.

Just once
I'd like to live a day in my own home
without being terrified.

Just once
I'd like to know that
when I shut the door
to my bedroom
or the bathroom,
it would stay shut.

Just once . . .
I'd like my wishes to come true.

....

Susie,
I'm sitting here in my room,
with the teddy bear on one side
and a box of Kleenex on the other.

Parents are asleep.
Charlie's tucked in.
Tim's on the phone.

My mind drifts back to those few weeks
I stayed with you after we returned from the tour.
You ironed my clothes when I was running late,
hugged me and got me off to work on time.

When I'd come in from cheer leading practice—
and you from a meeting with someone in our youth group—
we'd grab something to eat and just talk.
Sometimes we'd cry.

I loved the nights you came in with your guitar,
sat on the edge of my bed and sang.
That always seemed to calm my nerves.
So many times I told you to go away.

I'm glad you didn't.

When you finally put your guitar away and headed off to bed,
my heart was screaming, "No! Don't leave me."

Thanks for giving me your home when I needed it.
Though the pain never left, you gave me hope.

....

Emily,
I'm worried about you.
You never eat.
You average two hours of sleep each night.
You work a part-time job, and somehow you manage to stay involved in
school and church activities.

What's going to happen to you?
When will your breaking point come?
Someday will you just explode from all the pressure inside?

You work harder than anyone I know to make everyone
else believe your world is normal.
The class-favorite personality.
The cheerleader.
No one even suspects that you're breaking on the inside.
I'm worried about you.
You're becoming too good at acting.

....

God,
Why do You have to be our Father?
That name makes it so hard to trust You,
believe You and even want to love You.

Susie told me not to think of You as a man
but as some kind of spiritual being . . .our Creator and Sustainer
Someone who loves me more than I can imagine.
Someone who wants to take care of me forever.

But when I pray, I see Jesus. I know the Bible says
He is pure and godly, without sin, a miracle-worker.
But just when my prayers start to get through,
I remember that behind that white robe is the body of a man.
God, help me!

Susie,
You're probably wondering why I'm not at church tonight.
I didn't come . . . because I'm angry.

You always told me that if I said "I don't want to talk about it,"
I wouldn't have to. You always said that my body and
the details of my life were my choice to share or to keep.
Well, yesterday when you took me to the doctor, I said that.
Three times! She asked so many questions and didn't
back down when I said I didn't want to answer.

So I just gave short yes-no answers.
But by the end of the appointment, she ended up
knowing so much more than I intended.
Don't you understand how important
it is to me not to tell anybody?
It tears me up inside.

She wants me back in one week, so she can ask more questions.
Please understand why I can't go. I won't.

God,
In my office once again . . . planning retreats and mission trips
and the big discipleship kickoff next week. My mind is drifting. . . .

I catch myself glancing at my watch
and trying to remember what class Emily's in.
Picturing locker #219 and her stack of books all mixed together. Central
High School. Her world.

Home ec: Trying to visualize how far along her
dress is by now and how the material we picked out looks.

World literature: She called last night around 2:30 a.m. Said she couldn't
sleep because of the nightmare. Isn't ready for the book report that's due
today. Wondering if she'll be called on to report.

Trig: Supposed to have a test today. More tension to add to her already
pressure-filled world.

Health: Wondering if the open discussion is still on abuse, and if I'll be getting a phone call in a minute relaying the aloneness.

I want to intercede, Father.

Teach me how to help carry the weight.
When there are no more tears left for her to cry, let them fill my eyes.

When she can't find the words, help me seek them.

When she has no strength, allow me to stand in her place.

Show me how to make intercession a living reality.

....

Susie,
It's 11 p.m.
Company and family are all in bed.
I'm sitting here in the living room watching the lights
on the Christmas tree blink on and off.

Is it okay to say "I'm hurting"?

A couple of weeks ago, my counselor said,
"Don't deny your feelings. Let yourself feel."

But I'm scared to.
I feel like a little girl inside screaming,
"If I do, will you still love me?
Will you accept me when I look silly
with black mascara running down my face
and I can't talk because of the lump in my throat?"

I hurt so bad inside.
I'm so scared.
I'm all confused.

Will I ever be normal?

....

Susie,
You promised that you'd never make decisions
about my life . . . without me.
I begged . . .but you wouldn't give in.
Now, months later, I am in another
home with another family.

What have I done? Only bad kids are sent away.

Isn't it sad?

You've destroyed the very thing in me that you tried
to rescue me from . . .my freedom to make choices.

Emily,
Maybe someday you'll understand
why I had to involve other people.
Then again . . . maybe you'll never understand.

I realize I'm taking the risk of you turning on me forever. But can't you see
that my concern for you
goes way beyond how you feel toward me?

Your friendship is important to me.
But your emotional survival is more important.
I care whether you like or hate me—but I care more about you grabbing
hold of all the promise and potential wrapped within your future.
Ambivalence. Love me. Hate me. Cry on my shoulder.
Scream and walk away.
It doesn't change the fact that I'm committed to helping you. I'll wait this
thing out.
I'll continue to walk by your side . . .
even when you're angry.

Susie,
Why do you do it?
Over and over and over again,
through a calm voice and reassurance,
you pull out of me my painful memories
until I'm drowning in them.

For a while you feel them, too, the hurt and the confusion.
But then you can forget can go home.

I CAN'T!
Once again you've left me hurting.

Susie,
Looking back over the last six months . . .
you've been so positive and reassuring.
I appreciate you.
Thanks for always going that extra mile.

Susie,
Sometimes I wonder if I am his victim or yours. . . .

Victim to the manipulative way you talk me into
doing things I later regret for a lifetime.

Like talking with a social worker.
Like changing my home life forever.
I'm feeling so desperate to get away from you.
But because of the security you give that I need, I won't.
This time.

Emily,
Did you think I would merely listen and then forget?
Someone who would only wipe the tears away
for the time being and then send you on your way
with the empty promise of "things will get better"?

I had to do something.
How could I have lived with myself—
or even slept at night—
knowing that you were trapped in an inescapable prison?

Even you admitted to me that you could not survive
emotionally one more year in your situation.

I know I said I would never tell anyone.
I made a rash promise in desperation to comfort you.
It was an initial reaction made at midnight on tour.

I had no right to make a promise so bold.
I had no idea of the consequences or how tightly you were bound.

I quickly and impulsively made a promise I knew nothing about.

Will you forgive me?
I am so sorry, Emily.
Not for breaking the promise—
but for making a promise I couldn't keep.

Susie,
I can't describe how bad I feel
about the things I said to you last week.
So here I am on my 15-minute break with a Diet Coke, crying.
I am so sorry.

I feel guilty inside. And angry. And sad.
I feel like I'm being destroyed by
emotions that are out of my control.
Please stop this volcano.
I'm afraid I'm losing the battle.

Emily,
We were walking out of the judge's office.
You said nothing until we got to the car.
You turned to me with a look on your face that's frozen in my mind.

With a shaking voice you relayed what the judge had told you.

"She said that she wanted to put me in a home
situation where I would feel secure. Safe. A place
where I wouldn't have to worry about anything
else except what I would decide to wear to school the next day!

Your eyes filled with disbelief, and for the first time since I've known you, I
saw genuine hope stretch across your face.
It was as if the realization that "things really
don't have to be this way" had finally penetrated your thinking.

Then you looked at my with wonder.
"Susie, is that what other kids worry about?
What they'll wear to school?"

My heart splintered once again. I wanted to hold you like a child, wipe your
tears and somehow remove the tremendous burden you carried.

We started home.
You leaned against the car door and shut your eyes.
I stared at the road—my thoughts mixing with the traffic . . .

It's ironic. Most kids fight to be adults.
But you have to fight for the right just to be a kid.

Susie,
I've made progress this year because of you.
I'm glad God gave you to me.
But sometimes I still take steps backward.
For years, secrecy had become a way of life for me.
And even though we've made progress,
I want to run away from it all.
I want to hide.

Sometimes I think there is very little
that stands between me and insanity.
I feel bad if I tell. I feel bad if I don't.
I'm falling apart on the inside.

I can't see to grab hold of the fact
that I'm really worth something.
I wish security was an object-
something I could buy and hang on to.
Instead, it's something I have to work for.
Most of the time I feel like I don't even deserve to be secure.

How do I get over the self-hate?
It's not really ME I hate.
It's my body and what it can do.
Do you understand?

My past haunts me.
And I'm curious . . .will it ever leave me alone?

Emily,
A year ago, you dared to take the biggest risk in your life.
Sitting on a curb outside a hotel, you chose to break the silence that had
robbed you of childhood—the trauma that had made you a prisoner in your
own home.

Soon afterward came the pain of separation and the continual gnawing of
fear—wondering if you'd done the right thing by sharing such an enormous
secret.

But also came the opportunity to see the real YOU—a terrific young lady
discovering God's direction in her life, fully capable of making her own
decisions—and the realization that you deserve to add the phrases "I need"
and "I want" to your vocabulary.

I have never been naive enough to pretend I understand.
I've never said, "I know what you're going through."
I don't. Only you have the power to try to help me see inside.
I wish we could pretend that your past is simply a nightmare
that will fade after the morning has come and gone.
But this isn't just a bad dream, is it?

To say it's been a hard year is much more than an understatement.
You've been under another roof—lived with a different family—
left everything familiar, the only home you ever knew.

It was a matter of safety.
A question of emotional survival.
The desire for you to regain the control of your body
that was taken from you so long ago.
The need for you to realize that you are in control of you.
That you have the right to set limits and draw boundaries.
The necessity to know what is normal and what isn't.
And the need for you to be able to sleep at night
without the fear of being intruded upon.

This year brought many changes.
A new home. Counseling. Strained friendships. The fear of insanity.

But we have walked together. We have shared tears, lunches, prayers,
sunburns and giggles. We have talked into the wee hours of the morning,
made funnel cakes, tuna melts and solid memories.

When you told me your secret, I made an agape commitment to you—
a commitment of walking with you through the painful healing process,
and a commitment to keep you before our heavenly Father in consistent
prayer.

You see, Emily, when we base our security in a relationship with Jesus
Christ, He sets us free to love others. He guides us to invest our lives into
helping those around us draw closer to Him. He directs our time and
energies into making a life-time difference for someone.

Someday, you too will invest your life into patching up the broken heart of
another. And you'll do it not because it's part of your job, but because of
your growing relationship with the Lord.

As He changes your life, you'll help change someone else's.
God dreams BIG dreams for you, Emily.
I can't wait to hear from you . . . 10 years from now.

helping a friend who is struggling with sex

You may have a friend who's dealing with a sexual issue. Because there are so many varieties of issues that teens deal with on this topic, let's break it down to the top few areas of difficulty: Sexual Abuse; Incest; Rape; Teen Pregnancy; Homosexuality.

sexual abuse: incest

Studies suggest that one out of every four girls is sexually abused by someone in her family. For boys, the figure is one out of seven. Sexual activity among family members is called incest, and it's the most common type of sexual abuse.

Incest not only happens within *immediate* families but in *extended* families as well (stepparents, grandparents, uncles, stepbrothers, and so on).

Incest may be covert (concealed or less obvious) or overt (out in the open or blatant—something physical between two people). Jodie's uncle committed covert incest when he forced her to look at pornographic magazines. Anna's stepbrother committed covert incest when he took photos of her undressing. Tasha experienced overt incest when she was lone with her grandfather and he began touching her sexual organs.

It doesn't matter whether incest is covert or overt, it's still sexual abuse and is always a *crime*. Incest has been reported in every race of people in every era of time. If you have a friend who is a victim of incest, she's not alone. And neither is she at fault.

reaching out to a friend

It's likely that one of your friends at school or in your church youth group is trapped in an incestuous environment. If you suspect a friend is being sexually abused, look for these signs:

- Low self-esteem
- Difficulty in establishing proper relationships with the opposite sex (either completely withdrawn or promiscuous)
- Self-mutilation (cutting or burning herself)

[It doesn't matter whether incest is covert (concealed or less obvious) or overt (out in the open), it's still sexual abuse and is always a crime.]

- Reacts in a defensive manner when touched
- Dramatic changes in school performance
- Complains of frequent "general" pains
- Mood swings (happy one minute, sad the next)
- Severe depression
- Eating problems (Sexual abuse can lead to eating disorders, such as anorexia nervosa or bulimia. In fact, some researchers say that 80 percent of all eating disorders can be traced to sexual abuse.)
- Extreme hostility toward parents
- Overreacting to common problems
- Fearful of basements, closets or dark spaces
- Feeling unworthy of God's love and forgiveness
- Displaced anger (She's angry but directs her anger at the wrong person—maybe you!)

Though some of the above characteristics can result from her problems, if you notice that a friend displays *several* of them, it may be a sign that she's being sexually abused.

If you think one of your friends is being abused, it's time to consider sharing your suspicions with a trusted adult. But don't act *too* quickly—nobody likes rumors and misinformation about them spread around. In fact, the reputations of honest and totally innocent parents and families have been ruined because of false rumors and gossip.

Get the facts first. Gently approach your friend and ask a few leading questions. Let her know that you can be trusted. Remind her how much you care about her and value her friendship. She may not share her problem right away, but the important thing is that you stand by her—especially when she's angry or depressed.

"Praise be to the God and Father of our Lord Jesus Christ, the Father of compassion and the God of all COMFORT, who COMFORTS US in all our troubles, so that we can COMFORT THOSE in any trouble with the COMFORT WE OURSELVES HAVE RECEIVED from God."

(2 Corinthians 1:3-4)

breaking the silence

When your friend *does* decide to talk about her sexual abuse, realize that there's an immediate crisis the moment she tells you! Because you are now aware of the situation, things can never be the same again. By consciously choosing to share such a painful, personal part of her life with you, she is also choosing to break the conspiracy of silence.

It's important to realize that your friend has spent a long time building and maintaining a silent wall around this private area of her life. This intimate secret has been meticulously guarded. She will be very nervous about what you might do with this new information, so be extremely careful about how you proceed!

Try to express your concern in the following ways:

❶ **Thank her for sharing her secret with you.** Gently explain that you're not equipped to handle such a huge problem, but that you'll help her in any way you can.

❷ **Pray with her.** Remind her that God feels her pain. Memorize this verse together: "The Lord is close to the brokenhearted and saves those who are crushed in spirit" (Psalm 34:18).

❸ **Cry with her.** If you genuinely feel like crying, there's no need to hold back. Sometimes tears say a lot more than words. Let her know that you share her pain.

❹ **Listen, listen, listen.** The healing process begins when the secret is revealed, and your friend may want to talk about her experiences and her pain. If so, practice good listening skills—focus your entire attention on her, don't interrupt, maintain eye contact. If your friend isn't comfortable opening up, don't push or pry. She'll talk when she's ready.

❺ **Help her sort through the confusion, but don't give advice.** Your friend will probably be confused about a lot of things— her parents, her faith, her values and her feelings. For a while, she may feel that everything in her world is chaotic. YOU can be the one stable thing in her life, the one who points her to the Stabilizer Himself, Jesus Christ. Still, be careful not to give unasked-for advice. Your job is to be a friend, not to try to fix everything.

❻ **Don't walk out on her.** You may feel uncomfortable receiving such intimate and personal information. You might be embarrassed and nervous. That's all right—it's perfectly normal to feel that way. Whatever you do, though, don't ignore or avoid your friend or her problem. That would break her trust at the very time she needs it most.

For your friend, the hard stuff is just beginning.

Remembering (or sharing) an abusive situation is like a puzzle falling into place one piece at a time. As the experiences and emotions come together, she'll need a tremendous amount of support! Plan on being involved in her life the next several months or years.

➐ Point her toward qualified professionals. She may feel as though her whole life is a puzzle—but she'll also begin to realize that one important piece is missing. That piece is her childhood. She was robbed of a normal, healthy childhood. Like all of us who lose something important, she needs to grieve the loss. This means she needs a professional counselor to guide her through this process.

You are not equipped to help put her life back together. If you're a true friend, you'll help her find the right people to talk to.

➑ Don't make promises you can't keep. In trying to comfort and console your friend, you may be tempted to make promises you won't be able to live up to. Do not promise that you won't tell anyone. If her situation is to ever get better, you have to tell someone eventually!

This is not a secret for two teens to keep between themselves. A trusted adult must be brought into the situation or your friend will never get the help she needs and deserves. Before your friend even shares her problem with you, she might say, "I need to tell you something, but you have to promise you'll never tell anyone!" This should immediately clue you in to how frightened she is. Don't make that promise because you're curious and want to know what's bugging her. And don't make that promise because you feel sorry for her. A good response would be: "I care about you very much, and I want to help. I can tell something's bothering you, and it must be pretty important for you to want me to make such a bold promise. But because I care, I can't make that promise. I will, however, promise to stand by you. THAT you can count on."

➒ Be honest. While you don't want to make rash promises that you can't keep, you do want to offer honest comfort. Here are a few things you CAN say after she has shared her situation with you:

"Because I care about you, I cannot let you continue to be abused."

"Together, we need to decide how to get you the help you need."

"I will have to intervene."

"I am not trained or qualified to handle this situation by

myself. I want your permission to involve another person."

⑩ Be there. Your presence is far more important than having the right words to say or knowing exactly what to do. Sometimes there aren't any words that will comfort. Don't feel like you have to say just the right thing. Simply be with her. Be willing to sit right next to her in total silence for a couple of hours if that's what she needs. Your presence will speak volumes to your frightened, lonely friend.

jill's story

Jill works down the hall from me at Focus on the Family. She's an outgoing, beautiful young lady. You'd never guess that years of pain lie hidden behind her smile. Though she's never publicly shared the hurt she has experienced, she wants to offer hope to teen girls who may be trapped in incestuous homes. Therefore, she has decided to talk about her past right now.

If you have a friend who's being sexually abused, please ask her to read this. Here's Jill's story.

My parents divorced when I was only six months old. My mom abandoned me because I reminded her of my dad. She said I was a fat, ugly baby and didn't want anything to do with me. So I ended up at my grandmother's house—with my mom's mother. That's who raised me.

My grandmother was perfect on the outside. She and Grandpa had lots of money and could always afford the most fashionable clothes and the best of everything. We all went to church every Sunday, smiling on the outside but falling apart on the inside. You see, Grandma was mentally ill and emotionally abusive.

She constantly said hurtful things to me, such as, "We buy you such pretty clothes, but they look so horrible on you. Too bad you're not a pretty girl."

And she played weird mind games with me. For instance, she'd point to a red book and ask, "Jill, what color is that?"

"It's red, Grandma," I'd say.

Then she'd start screaming and violently insist that it was blue. She'd point her finger at me and yell, "You're an idiot, Jill! You're so stupid!" This would go on and on until I'd finally give in and agree that it was blue.

You can imagine after years of this, I began to see the world around me in her abnormal way. I learned not to trust what I perceived as reality, but to accept her reality instead. Soon I began believing that I really was fat, useless and ugly.

Grandma was extremely controlling. She read all my letters and monitored all my phone calls. I had no privacy. My entire world revolved around whatever she wanted it to be.

feeling trapped

When I was 13 years old, my grandpa died, and it seemed as though something snapped inside my grandmother, making her even crazier. Her brother—my great-uncle—began coming around. She said it was because Uncle Mac wanted to represent a father figure to me.

He started picking me up after school and taking me to movies and fancy, four-star restaurants. One evening as we walked to his car, he cornered me between another car and a wall. I was shocked when he slid his hand up my shorts. I pushed him away and screamed, "What are you doing?"

But he grabbed me and pushed me against the car, pressing his body close to mine and rubbing himself against me. I felt dirty and ashamed. I began thinking it was all my fault. I shouldn't have worn these shorts, I thought. I'm so stupid! I must have given him some kind of signal or something.

Even though I blamed myself for what had happened, I knew that what he had done was wrong. I'm not sure how I knew; I just knew it.

When I got home, Grandma was standing at the kitchen sink, washing dishes. I told her exactly what had happened. She was furious! She pulled a wet plate out of the sink and hurled it at me while screaming, "You're a liar! You're a no-good liar, Jill!"

Then she locked me in my bedroom for two days. The only time I was allowed to come out was to use the bathroom. I received no food and no water. She said I wouldn't be released from my room until I admitted that I had lied.

Finally, I couldn't stand being a prisoner in my bedroom any longer. I gave in just to be able to eat and get dressed and walk around the house. She then called Uncle Mac and told him to come over because I had something to tell him.

I was then forced to apologize for what I had said. I had to tell him that I lied, and I had to agree to continue seeing him.

Even though I blamed myself for what had happened, I knew that what he had done was wrong. I'm not sure how I knew; I just knew it.

other problems

By the time I was in high school, I had developed bulimia. Oftentimes, eating disorders can be traced to abuse. I realized that my great-uncle had sexually abused me, but I didn't realize that I was being emotionally abused by Grandma. She was constantly telling me I was fat, stupid and worthless. I knew she was mentally ill. and it was obvious that she was mean and controlling, but I didn't know this was considered emotional abuse.

Controlling my food intake was one way that I could take charge. Subconsciously, I wanted to control my own life and my own body. No one else could dictate what I would eat or wouldn't eat. I wanted everything on the outside to look as perfect as possible in order to make up for how lousy I felt on the inside.

Right before my high school graduation, Grandma told me that she knew where my dad was. I hadn't been in contact with him at all, so you can imagine my surprise to learn his whereabouts! She allowed me to send him a graduation announcement. He attended the graduation and even treated me to dinner.

We really clicked. I loved being with him, and he seemed so sympathetic and understanding. He had learned—even through the short time he was married to my mom—what my grandma was like. I felt I had finally found an understanding friend. We promised to keep in touch after I got to college.

As I left for college, I was totally unprepared for living and relating in a normal world. It was hard for me to make good decisions. I had to depend a lot on what others told me, because I had spent years with an abusive relative pounding false reality into my brain.

I started dating a guy who was also emotionally abusive. Thinking back on it, maybe I was drawn to him because that's what I was used to. I found out later that he was a serial rapist on our campus. He stood in front of the dorms and studied the freshman girls going in and out. He watched them long enough that he could tell which ones struggled with low self-esteem. Naturally, I was an easy target.

He befriended me and started the relationship by showering me with kindness. But it wasn't too long before he began being extremely possessive. He isolated me until he was the only person I saw, and he began controlling my life. Again, since I was used to this from living with my grandma, it all seemed normal.

bad news

One night he called and canceled our date, so I went out to eat with a girlfriend. It just so happened that we spotted him at the same restaurant with another girl. I was furious! I told him I never wanted to see him again.

Later, he phoned me while drunk and began calling me every horrible name in the book. I held my ground, though, and said it was over. A couple of days passed, and he called again—asking if we could talk. I turned him down and repeated that we were finished.

A few hours later, I heard a knock on my door. I thought it was the girl down the hall returning some books I had loaned her. I opened the door and saw him instead.

He was extremely apologetic and nice, and even though I knew I shouldn't, I let him in. When he began talking about getting back together, I continued to stand my ground. "We can't," I said. "It's over. I don't want to go out with you anymore."

He became angry and started screaming at me, so I told him to leave. "Then open the door and let me out!" he yelled.

I stepped past him to turn the doorknob, but as I did, he grabbed me from behind. He threw me down and raped me. I screamed, but no one could hear because he held a pillow over my face.

I reported it to the campus police, and they questioned him, but he had made up an alibi. He had some friends say that he was in his room the entire time.

Two days later, as I was coming out of a night class, he jumped out of the bushes and beat me up. He tore a muscle in my back and dislocated my vertebrae. I was in a wheelchair for six weeks.

"If you don't drop the charges," he threatened, "I'll kill you."

I knew he meant business, and I was scared to death! He began stalking me—no matter what time it was or where I was, he was there. After several weeks, I was such an emotional wreck that I dropped the charges.

a downward spiral

When I went back to Grandma's house in June, I was really restless. I had tasted freedom while away at college, and I didn't like being in her emotionally unstable and controlling environment any longer. I was also still trying to get over the rape, and I just needed a friend.

A college pal who lived a couple of hours away invited me to come spend a week with her family. Grandma said I could go, and I excitedly packed enough clothes for seven days. This is exactly what I need, I thought. Then for some unknown reason, on the day I was supposed to leave, Grandma changed her mind.

"If you leave for a week, I'll make sure you leave for good!" she snarled. She started throwing my belongings everywhere. I was so tired of all the violence in my life that I decided to go ahead and leave, even though I knew I would never have a home with her again.

I ended up coming back in two days, and my room was totally empty. All my possessions were gone! It was as if I had never existed. I told Dad what was going on, and he invited me to come stay with him and his wife.

Two weeks after I moved in with Dad, he started molesting me. It started with simple touching. He began touching me underneath my nightgown while saying, "You have nowhere else to go. I'm all you have. Just relax and go along with this, or you'll have nothing!" The abuse progressed from his touching me to him forcing me to touch him. From there, the abuse got worse and worse, until finally, he started having intercourse with me.

Eventually, I moved out of my dad's house, putting an end to the abuse, and finished my college degree. Breaking out of the abusive situation was the first step toward healing.

putting the pieces back together

The hopeful news I want to share with you is that the friend you're seeking to help can overcome an abusive background and find healing and wholeness!

All my life, I continued going to church, reading my Bible and depending on God's guidance to get me through the traumatic times. And you know? Even though life wasn't fair, God was always there. He provided the strength I needed to carry on despite the abuse, and He walked with me through the nightmares.

I began going to counseling a year ago, and I'm getting stronger every day. God is helping me heal, and I now know He can make something beautiful out of anything! Through counseling and with God's help, I'm putting myself back together again. I'm slowly learning that I can trust my own view of reality. I'm becoming one person—whole and free! The path to healing has, indeed, been long and difficult. But the good news is that there's hope for anyone who has been abused.

Counseling is often hard work. It's not easy to talk about the pain

I was so tired of all the violence in my life that I decided to go ahead and leaave, even though I knew I would never have a home with her again.

and hard times I've experienced. But healing is so important to me that sharing the hurt is worth it. There's no way I could do with without God. He gives me hope and fills my life with purpose and meaning.

I'm now 33 years old, and God has blessed me with a terrific Christian husband and two great children. It's taken a while, but I've finally learned that my self-worth doesn't come from what other people say about me. For years I thought I was no good because the people closest to me kept telling me how rotten I was.

I now know that my self-image comes from being unconditionally loved and totally accepted by God. Can you imagine how free that makes me feel? I don't have to live in the past anymore! I don't have to dwell on trying to understand why this or that happened. I can simply relax and bask in His great, overflowing love for me.

What about you? Do you have a friend who has been sexually abused? Have you experienced sexual abuse? Though it may seem impossible, I want you to know that you CAN get your life back. You CAN become the young lady God intends for you to be. Please believe me—there IS life after abuse.

I hope you can help your friend realize that help is available. Your local phone book will have several hot line numbers listed on the inside front cover. Consider calling one of those numbers or one of the following:
- Abuse Registry 1-800-962-2873
- Child Abuse/Family Violence 1-800-422-4453
- Focus on the Family (ask for the counseling department) 1-800-232-6459
- Minirth Meier New Life Clinics 1-800-NEW-HOPE

Through counseling and with God's help, I'm putting myself back togehter again. I'm slowly learning that I can trust my own view of reality. I'm becoming one person—whole and free!

sexual abuse:
rape and date rape

Since the majority of teen girls who are raped, are raped by someone they know, this section will focus more on date rape than rape itself. Helping a friend who has been sexually abused by someone she knows will be similar in helping someone who has been sexually abused by a stranger.

Before we talk about how to help a friend who has experienced date rape, though, let's first concentrate on rape.

Even though you and your friends may think, *That would never happen to me,* it's wise to take precautions. Here are a few tips you can share with a friend who's concerned about the possibility of rape happening to her.

- When shopping at the mall, always park your car near a light or as close to the building as possible.
- Carry mace spray or a whistle with you at all times that's easily accessible.
- If possible, try not to be alone in secluded areas (parking lot, jogging alone, hiking, etc.).
- Listen to your senses. If you "feel" something's wrong, it very well could be. Leave the area immediately.
- Always lock the car doors when driving—even in daylight.

if it happens to a friend

When a friend is raped, she may withdraw or go into denial and try to pretend nothing ever happened. Neither of these options are healthy choices. If you suspect your friend has been raped, let her know beyond all doubt that you're here to help.

And the best help you can give her is getting her to report what happened. Rape is a crime! Your friend is a victim. As much as she would like to simply take a shower, throw her soiled clothes away and try to forget the nightmare ever occurred, the smartest thing to do would be to go immediately to the police.

Once reported, the police will arrange for her to be examined by a doctor who will also report his findings. Even though she may feel like she's having to go through interrogation just to report a crime, she'd actually be helping someone else—a future victim—by trying to put a stop to the man who violated her.

Why is it so important to be examined by a doctor? Because of the danger of sexually transmitted diseases (STDs) and the possibility of pregnancy. Even though your friend won't want to tell a police officer the details of her experience or be seen by a doctor, it really is in her best interest to do so. And you can help by involving her parents, staying with her and encouraging her.

date rape

Dear Susie:

The hottest guy in school asked me out. I was really excited, because every single girl is love with him. He asked me to our football homecoming. After the game, we went to a party where alcohol was being served. I didn't really want to go, but I didn't know how to say no.

He started drinking and offered me a drink, too. I declined, but he kept pressuring me. Everyone else was drinking, so I finally gave in. I really didn't have that much, but I wish I hadn't taken any.

After about an hour, he suggested we leave. He drove me to a secluded area and started getting physical with me in the parked car. I was really uncomfortable. He'd had way too much to drink, and I kept telling him I didn't want to do this. But he only got more forceful.

I finally slapped him and pushed him off of me, but that only made him angry. He forced me to have sex with him.

I feel so betrayed and hurt. I don't know what to do. If I tell my parents, I'll get in major trouble for drinking and for parking. Help!

Cyndi

What Cyndi has just described is date rape—sometimes it's called acquaintance rape. You may have heard several myths about date rape. Let's look at a few myths and dispel them with the truth, so you'll be better equipped to help a hurting friend.

Myth: "It would never happen to me."
Truth: Date rape (as well as rape) can happen to *anyone*. No one can be guaranteed absolute safety.

Myth: "It wouldn't happen to me, because I always know the guys I date."
Truth: Even guys you know can have a night and day change when they start drinking.

Myth: "I wouldn't go out with anyone who would hurt me."
Truth: No one says to herself, "I think I'll go out with Ryan— he seems dangerous."

Myth: "I have great instincts. I'd be able to tell if a guy had that on his mind."
Truth: "How can we tell what *anyone* has on his mind? None of us are mind-readers! And our instincts aren't 100 percent correct all the time."

more truth

Every single minute, 1.3 women are raped in the United States. That equals 78 rapes every hour, 1,872 rapes every day, 56,160 rapes every month and 683,280 rapes every year. (These are reported cases only.) Don't assume you and your friends are not in danger.

about date rape

- Rapists aren't always strangers.
- Date rape is about power, control and anger. It's *not* about passion or romance.
- When someone you know forces you to have sex—it's still considered rape as much as if that person were a stranger.
- Date rape is a serious crime. It's a betrayal of trust and leaves emotional scars.

Every single minute, 1.3 women are raped in the United States. That equals 78 rapes every hour, 1,872 rapes every day, 56,160 rapes every month and 683,280 rapes every year.

DO:
- Trust your gut feelings. Though our instincts aren't 100 percent right all the time, it's better to err on the side of being to cautious than by being too trusting. If your date is making you feel uneasy, call it off. Or if the place he's taken you makes you uncomfortable, leave.
- Stay completely away from alcohol and drugs.
- Know the guy you go out with, as well as his friends and family if possible.
- Take money with you for an emergency phone call or taxi.
- Stay in public places.

DON'T:
- Leave a party, game or concert with someone you just met or someone you don't know very well.
- Continue to go out with a guy who puts you down.
- Date guys who try to control you, your choice of friends or the way you dress.

helping a friend

If you have a friend who has experienced date rape, she'll have a confusing array of feelings—anger, fear, depression, humiliation and lack of trust in others.

She may also try to blame herself:
— "I should have worn something different."
— "I must have given out some signals I wasn't aware of."
— "If only I would have been more careful."

Remind your friend that when a girl says no, her word should be taken as her word. *No one* has the right to cross boundaries that she has established for herself. Let her know over and over that if she said no and she's feeling guilty, she's feeling false guilt. Remind her that you love her and believe in her.

Encourage your friend to get professional help. Though you can give her tons of emotional support, you are not equipped to help her deal with the pain. Call your local rape crisis line for immediate help, and they'll help you get in touch with a professional therapist.

Don't let your friend isolate herself. This will only prolong her pain. She needs to deal with it, but she needs professional help to deal with it.

She also needs to be examined by a physician—immediately. Don't let her shower, wash or change clothes. Valuable evidence could be destroyed.

Believe your friend. Give her as much comfort and support as you can. Go with her to the hospital, police station or counseling center. Keep repeating that she is not to blame!

why does date rape happen?

Here are a few reasons I believe this crime is even happening today:

1. Our society is obsessed with sexualized violence in the media. (Think about some of the most popular movies being advertised. People flock to see movies with rape and violence.)
2. Pornography reinforces the myth that women want sex even when they say no or if it's painful.
3. Men are often taught to be aggressive and masculine. Unfortunately, this often includes the pressure to score from peers and to pursue fun. Women are brought up to be feminine. They want romance, and they want to find "Mr. Right." This creates a situation where the man is the predator and the woman is the prey.
4. Sexual violence is also a product of society's strong endorsement of drinking alcohol. "You're not a real man unless you drink." Seventy-five percent of all date rapes involve alcohol or drugs. Think of all the beer commercials and how many of them target teen guys.

date rape facts

Fact: Only one percent of all date rapes are ever reported.
Fact: Fifty-seven percent of all rapes happen on dates.
Fact: One out of three women will be sexually assaulted in their lifetime.
Fact: Several studies have shown that pornography desensitizes men to sexual violence and rape.
Fact: These same studies also conclude that porn has an addictive quality and that men who become addicted have a need for more graphic and violent pornography.
Fact: Date rape is never the victim's fault. They may find them-

selves in a dangerous situation because of poor judgment, but no one has the right to violate your body even if they have become aroused.

Fact: Taking sex from someone does not lead to intimacy, and it's not an achievement to be proud of with friends.

what does a date rapist look like?

Of course, no one can draw a picture of all men who will rape someone in their lives, but there *are* some common characteristics you can watch out for:

- They begin having sex at an earlier age.
- They tend to talk about sex a great deal.
- They feel sex is an achievement, and it makes them feel important, powerful and in control.
- They are con artists who use only a moderate amount of force.
- They usually have poor communication skills with the opposite sex.
- They are almost always into pornography, whether it's magazines, videos, the computer, music or all of the above.

what you can do

Obviously, you can't stop date rape from happening. But you *can* encourage your friends to set high standards for themselves by being an example and setting high standards for *yourself.* Here are my suggestions:

Date Christians. I realize that anyone can say he's a Christian, and sometimes Christian guys are more "handsy" than nonbelievers. But set a high standard for your dates. Decide now to only date solid Christian guys. If you're not sure about his spiritual status, don't go out with him.

And if there aren't any Christian guys in your small town? Take advantage of this time to deepen your relationship with Christ. You may not date until you get to college. You may not date until you're out of college. It's okay. You won't fold up and die. I promise.

Know the guy well. And don't settle for simply knowing *him.* What's his family like? What church do they attend? How does he treat his parents? His brothers and sisters?

Date someone with similar values. If you don't go to dances, why date someone who does? Try to date guys who won't question your standards, but guys who will respect them and help you maintain those standards.

Pray about your dating relationships. This is the most important thing you can do! And even though it might feel weird, I hope you'll also begin praying right *now* for your husband. I realize you don't even have a clue who that will be yet, but go ahead and start praying for him. In fact, let's do it right now, okay?

Dear Jesus,
Thanks for the man you have selected for me. I don't want anything less than Your choice for my lifetime mate. Help me to be patient and to wait on Your timing.

Father, whoever he is . . . be close to him right now. Help him to grow strong in You. Give him good Christian friends who will encourage his relationship with You.

Help him to establish high standards and to maintain them. Strengthen him, Father. Help him not to yield to temptation. Keep him pure.

Help him begin developing now into the godly man I'll need someday. And help me to begin developing into the godly woman he'll someday need. Keep me pure, Jesus. I trust You with my future and with all my relationships.
Amen.

pregnancy

Dear Susie:
Todd and I had been dating for seven months. He told me he loved me, and I believed him. I loved him, too. We started sleeping together when his parents weren't home. I never thought it would happen to me, but . . . now I'm pregnant.

I'm not very far along. In fact, I'm not even showing yet. But I bought one of those pregnancy tests from the store, and it showed that I'm pregnant.

I told Todd, and he dumped me. He said I should have been more careful—that I should have been taking something.

I can't believe this! I'm only 16 years old. I'm on the volleyball team at school. I feel like my life is over! I can't tell my parents. They're Christians, and they'd die. Please help me!
Courtney

what to do

First things first. When your friend shares this kind of secret with you, pray! The best thing you can do is pray with her at that very moment. Choosing to participate in sex outside of marriage is a sin. She needs to repent and seek God's forgiveness. And the exciting thing about our heavenly Father is the fact that He *will* forgive her! She can start all over.

Though there will be consequences that she'll need to deal with, she can still live a victorious and joyful life in Christ. You can help her realize that by praying with her and by listening to her pray.

her parents

Though she may not want to tell her folks, you'll need to encourage her to do so. They really need to be a part of the next nine months *with* her. They may or may not be supportive, but they still need to know.

medical help

After she has told her parents, hopefully they'll begin to guide and help her with the medical attention she'll need. If, by chance, they disown her or refuse to help her, *you* step up to the plate and prove what friendship is all about.

If she can't afford to see her family physician, take her to the county health department. It's important that she get medical attention early, because: (1) The health of the baby is at stake and (2) her health is at stake (she needs to be examined for STDs).

her options

Your local Crisis Pregnancy Center can be an extremely valuable place to turn to! You can find them in the Yellow Pages of the phone directory. They're experienced volunteers and can help your friend with decisions she'll need to make.

What are her choices? I sincerely hope your friend won't even consider abortion as an option. I believe abortion is murder. If she chooses to give the baby up for adoption, there are thousands of childless couples waiting in line to receive a newborn.

If you don't go to dances, why date someone who does? Try to date guys who won't question your standards, but guys who will respect them and help you maintain those standards..

if she starts dating again

Chances are she'll become involved sooner or later in another dating relationship. You can help your friend not repeat the same mistake by encouraging her to establish firm boundaries for herself and holding her accountable to those boundaries.

- Date only Christian guys.
- Don't spend prolonged time alone with him.
- Strive to group date as much as possible.
- Stay in public areas
  (miniature golf, bowling, tennis, shopping, etc.).
- Have a plan before the date actually begins: Know where you're going and how much time it will take. This way, you won't have two extra hours at the end of your date with nothing to do. That's what gets many teens in trouble.
- Stick with the plan.

how to Help your hurting friend

SECTION 3

letters to Susie

Dear Susie:
I have a friend who's into palm reading. He read a book about it and how to do it, and now he's reading everybody's palms in class. I told him I think it's wrong, but I can't tell him why, because I don't know if or where the Bible says that.
Heidi

Dear Heidi:
God comes out very strongly against occult activities in Leviticus 20:27. Here it is: "A man or woman who is a medium or spiritist among you must be put to death. You are to stone them; their blood will be on their own heads."

Yikes! That pretty much erases all doubt, doesn't it? Of course, that was written in the Old Testament—before Jesus came to die *for* our sins, so we wouldn't have to.

Because of His death on the Cross, we can seek His forgiveness for our sins, and accept that forgiveness and live in victory. So, if your friend were to accept Christ as his Savior and repented of his involvement in palm reading, God would immediately forgive him. (Aren't you glad Jesus paid the death penalty for our sins! It's nothing to take for granted, is it?)

Yes, God comes out strongly against occult activity and throughout the Bible forbids people from participating in it. This not only includes palm reading, but astrology, fortune-telling, seances

> "May the Lord make your love **INCREASE** and **OVERFLOW** for each other."
> (1 Thessalonians 3:12)

and ouija boards as well. In the Bible, a person who performed these kinds of practices was called a medium or a spiritist. When King Saul fell away from God, he became involved with a medium. Read the whole story in 1 Samuel , chapter 28. It's a frightening portrait of depending on power other than God's.

If we want spiritual victory in our lives, we are to depend on God's power only. Anything else is a lie straight from hell.

I don't advise pointing your finger at your friend. I think he's simply confused and isn't aware of the wonderful saving power of Jesus Christ. I encourage you to be kind to him, gently explain God's stand against all forms of the occult and leave the rest up to God.

You may also want to contact the following ministries for suggestions on witnessing to someone involved in the occult:

Christian Research Institute (CRI)
P.O. Box 7000
Rancho Santa Margarita, CA 92688-7000

Spiritual Counterfeits Project
P.O. Box 4308
Berkeley, CA 94704

Dear Susie:

I have a problem I need help with. My friend has been extremely depressed. She told me she thinks she should be in pain, so she constantly cuts herself. She has gone to some doctors to find out why she's so depressed, but so far, they don't know.

She was doing better for a while, but now it's really bad. And she slept with her boyfriend, which I know doesn't help. She told me she has given up on God and doesn't want to get better, but I can tell she's screaming for someone to help.

I don't know what to do. I pray continually and have encouraged her and given her Bible verses, but I'm at the end of my rope.

Stacia

Dear Stacia:

I'm impressed with your sensitive and compassionate heart. I'm glad she's seen a doctor, but it sounds like the cause of her problems haven't been determined yet. As mentioned in Section

Two, "cutters" are dealing with some major hurt inside.

You mentioned that you've been praying for her. Please pray *with* her as well—if she'll let you. As much as you want to help her and give her some answers, you're limited because you're her friend. She really needs professional help. Will you encourage her to see a counselor? Offer to go with her if she's afraid to go alone.

Let her know you're always ready to listen. And encourage her to read Chava's story in Section Two. I'm glad she has *you* for a friend.

Dear Susie:
My friend has cancer, and I feel at a loss for words. I want to minister to her and keep being her friend, but I'm not sure how.
Katrina

Dear Katrina:
If I were battling cancer, you're exactly the kind of friend I'd want by my bedside! I admire your tenderness.

There are times when words simply can't express what we're feeling. It sounds like this is the case between you and your friend. Probably the very best way you can minister to her is simply to be near her. If she's not in too much pain, you may want to hug her gently or hold her hand.

If she wants to talk, be willing to listen. Ask if she has a favorite book she'd like you to read out loud for her. Or maybe she has some Scripture underlined in her Bible that you could read to her. Be willing to do anything necessary, but also learn to be comfortable doing nothing but simply being together. God bless you!

Dear Susie:
One of my friends listens to Korn but preaches about how she's going to save herself until she's married. It makes me mad because it's unfair. I don't listen to it, and I'm saving myself too. She's a cafeteria Christian—picking around at various churches for a friendlier religion. What can I do to help?
Tori

Dear Tori:
The beginning point in witnessing to an unbeliever is a consistent and sincere expression of unconditional love and respect. Don't get into arguments with her. You may win a battle but eventually lose the war.

You lifestyle shouts volumes! Ask God to give you opportunities to gently share His truth with her. He knows exactly what your friend needs to hear. While you'd probably love to hurry the whole thing up and get her "right with Christ" immediately, remember that God's timing is perfect. She may not come to know Him overnight, but let's trust God that she'll eventually give herself 100 percent to His authority.

Meanwhile, since she's into Korn, how about offering her some Christian music that has a close sound? Most Christian bookstores now have listening centers so you can actually hear a CD before you purchase it. Ask the clerk to help you find similar sounds for your friend.

And about her virginity: I hope she *does* wait until marriage. It sounds as though you're frustrated because she's being hypocritical saying she'll save herself for her husband—but at the same time will fill her ears with music that blasts all kinds of sexual perversion. Yes, that *is* hypocritical.

But remember, anyone can say no to sexual intercourse. That doesn't make someone a Christian. Philippians 3:18 tells us that many who call themselves Christians are really enemies of the Cross. And we're told in 1 Timothy 3:16 that it's not easy to live a godly life.

We learn in 2 Timothy 3:1 that it's going to be really tough to be a Christian in the last days. The Bible also describes your friend's desire to be a "cafeteria Christian"—picking and choosing what she wants to believe. The New Testament warns us that in the last days people in the church won't want to hear the truth. They'll become upset at good, holiness preaching, because it will make them uncomfortable. So they'll leave that church go to another, hoping to hear something that will tickle their ears.

Your friend is confused right now, but the good news is that she's searching. Keep loving her—even when you want to scream at her—and trust Christ to give you continued opportunities to share His love and truth with her.

Dear Susie:

My best friend and I had a huge blowout. She's been mad at me for a whole month now. And . . . I'm pretty ticked off at her, too. She let something slip that I shared with her in confidence. That really hurt! I'm afraid our friendship is damaged forever.

Jacki

Dear Jacki:

Your friendship doesn't *have* to be damaged forever. It's up to you. Will you decide to forgive and forget? I realize you've been terribly hurt . . . but you've probably let things slip before, too. No one's perfect—not you and not even your best friend.

I always think it's sad when two good friends let a misunderstanding come between them. Be bigger than the problem, Jacki. There's only one Person who can help heal the hurt inside you and give you the ability to forgive: Jesus Christ. Wanna talk with Him about it right now?

God Said...I Said
This is a private conversation.
DON'T READ...unless you
enjoy eavesdropping.

God Said: You miss her, don't you?

I Said: Alison?

Yes.

Ah, not really.

Hmmm.
Not even walking to school together?

Nah.
It's kind of nice being alone.
Gives me time to think.

Not even having lunch
together in the school cafeteria?

It's probably better that
I eat faster anyway;
it gives me time to leave and
get started on my homework.

And what about youth group?

Well, I'm still going
to Sunday school.
I guess it's not that important
that I go to youth group all the time.
I wouldn't want to go and be
there with Alison.
It would feel too awkward.

Isn't it awkward *now*—
holding this grudge against her?

Well . . . yeah . . .
things are weird. But . . .
it would be even
weirder to forgive her.

Or would it?

Huh?

Just how long do you plan
on trying to avoid her? Eating alone.
Hanging out by yourself.
Missing youth group.
Wouldn't it be easier to simply
forgive her and get on with your life?

No.

Are you sure?

Positive.

Hmmm.
Remember the time you
lied to your mom about
breaking your curfew?

That was over a year ago!
You sure have a good memory.

I'm God. I know everything.

Oh, yeah. Okay, so what's the deal?
Why are You suddenly
changing the subject
from Alison to my curfew?
That has absolutely nothing to do
with how she hurt me.

The point is, you lied.
But I forgave you.

Well, that wasn't hard to forgive.
It was only curfew!

My child, any time you lie,
you're being deceptive—
and that goes directly against
My holy character. It hurts Me.

Hurts You? Nah.
Murder—that hurts You.
And children starving.
That's gotta hurt.
And Your heart probably breaks
every time someone is abused.
But stretching the
truth about curfew?
Nah, that can't hurt.

When you lie, My child,
you're breaking one of the
Ten Commandments.
You're going directly against

"He who GUARDS his LIPS
guards his SOUL, but he who
speaks rashly will come to ruin."

(Colossians 3:17)

My plan for your life.
You're sinning. Every sin—
murder, abuse, stealing, gossip,
lying—they *all* hurt Me.
And they hurt deeply.
I *died* so that you wouldn't
have to pay the
penalty for those sins.

I'm sorry, Father.
I guess I just wasn't
thinking that stretching the truth
about my curfew was really a sin.
But, You're right.
Any time I choose to
deceive someone, I'm lying.
I'm so sorry, God.

I know you are. I know your heart.
It's tender. I have forgiven you.

Whew! That sure feels good.

But we're not finished.

Well, yeah we are.
You know I'm sorry.
And I've accepted
Your forgiveness.

But we're still not finished.
What about Alison?

Oh, man!
Why did You have
to bring *her* up again?

Because she's My child,
and I love her deeply.
I died for her, too, you know.

But, God! She really hurt me.
She *really* hurt me!
I mean . . . You have no idea.

Oh, I know all about hurt.
Two of my own disciples
betrayed me. One sold me

for a lousy 30 pieces of silver.
My *life* for 30 pieces of silver!
And the other one—
one whom I had
nicknamed "The Rock" and
said I'd build My church on—
lied and said he didn't
know Me—had never
even heard of Me. Yes,
My child, I know all about hurt.

Yeah, but Judas
was a weirdo from
the very beginning.
Alison's not a weirdo.
What I'm going through
doesn't even compare
to a couple of disciples—
especially since Peter
got back on good terms
with You—and Judas
was such a flake.

Flake? Weirdo? The day
before I selected my 12 disciples,
I had spent the entire night
praying about whom to choose.
None of them were chosen flippantly.
Judas was chosen to follow Me,
because he was stacked with
talent and ability. He showed promise
and possessed such an eagerness.
He wasn't weird.
He was good with numbers.
He was dependable.
The other disciples trusted
him enough to put him in charge of
our financial funds. Yes, he eventually
betrayed Me, but it didn't happen overnight.
He slowly began backing away
emotionally and spiritually before
he ever made his physical move of betrayal.
I know about hurt.

Yeah, but it all turned out okay.

Okay?

Well, yeah. I mean, he killed himself.
So You never had to think about it again.
I'm always running into Alison,
and the hurt is fresh every time I see her!

My heart broke for Judas.
If only he would have sought me
out before hanging himself.
If only he would have found Me.

Why? What difference
would that have made?

A lot. You see, My child,
I would have forgiven him—
if only he would have asked.

Forgiven him? *Forgiven him?*
He betrayed You, Father!
How could You have forgiven him?

He's not the only one
who has betrayed Me.

Well, yeah . . . Peter.
But he sought forgiveness.

Peter and Judas aren't the
ones I'm thinking of right now.

Well, who else, God?

You, My child.

Me?!?

You.

Oh, Father!
Please don't say that!
I'd never betray You.

When you refuse to forgive
someone who has hurt you,
you're betraying Me.

No!

I want you to forgive Alison.

I can't, God!
It hurts too much!

I understand. I know all about hurt.
And when *you* hurt, I hurt.
I've cried the tears with you.
You've never been alone.

But, God, it's just not fair!
She promised she'd
never tell anyone.

> I know all about hurt. And when you hurt, I hurt.
> I've cried the tears with you. You've never been alone.

letters to
SUSIE **119**

I trusted her. I wouldn't tell
just *anyone* who I like.
And she gave me her word
she'd never tell.
Then she had to
go and blab it to
Justin that I think he's hot.
How could she?
I've never been so
embarrassed in my entire life!

I understand. I created you,
and I know how badly your
heart is bruised right now.
But, I promise . . .
it's not the end of the world.

It sure feels like it!

And even though Alison
broke a promise, she never
really betrayed you.

What?!?

She was trying to get Justin
to ask you to the
cook-out next week.

What?!?

She thought if he
knew you liked him,
he'd have the confidence
he needed to ask you.

What?!?

It's true.

Well . . . what . . .
she . . . I mean . . . how . . .

She *did* break a promise—
and I know you're hurting over that.
And she *did* tell Justin
something that you're wishing
he didn't know. But she didn't
do it out of spite. Believe it or not,
she was trying to help. Granted,
she didn't think it through.
Yes, she should have talked
it over with you—asked your
permission. But she wasn't
out to hurt you. That was not her motive.

"Pride only breeds quarrels,
but WISDOM is found
in those who take advice."
(Proverbs 13:10)

I never knew.

Because you never asked.

She should have told me.

She tried. But it's hard to
hear when you're running
away while she's talking.

Well . . . I didn't know.

You reacted out of hurt,
instead of expecting
the best in her.

It still hurts.

I know.

And I'm still embarrassed.

I realize that. But if I can forgive
those who have wronged Me,
shouldn't you also forgive
those who break your trust?

Yeah, probably.

Could you be a little more definite?

But I'm still angry!
And I don't think it's
fair that I should have
to forgive her. After all, she
did promise. She broke her
promise, God!

And I know your hurt.
But the bottom line is this:
You'll break one of
your promises to Me
sometime in the next
couple of weeks.
Should I forgive you?

Well, sure, God!
You know my heart.
You know I love You.
And yeah, sometimes I blow it,
but my relationship with
You is important to me.

I always ask You for forgiveness
when I know I've gone
against Your will.

My child . . .
if you don't forgive
those who hurt you,
it stands in the way
of My bestowing
forgiveness upon *you.*

But, God!
You can't hold this against me!
Alison hurt me.

And you'll hurt *Me.*

You've gotta forgive
me when I blow it.
I'm just 16! I don't always
realize I'm even *doing*
something that hurts
You until I'm right in the
middle of doing it.
But I'm always sorry!

I know You are.
I know your heart.

Okay, then.

But I also know
Alison's heart. And I know
that she's sorry about the
embarrassment she's
caused you. She loves you.
She treasures your friendship.
You two have a lot of great
memories together.
I want you to forgive her.
By extending your forgiveness
to her, it keeps your heart
uncluttered and allows
My forgiveness to
flow freely to *you.*

Wow. I never thought of it
that way before. It's really
pretty complicated, isn't it?

Well, it *sounds* complicated.

No, not really.

It's simply a decision

[By extending your forgiveness to her, it keeps your heart
uncluttered and allows My forgiveness to flow freely in you.]

to allow Me to be Lord of
your life. Not just your
future, your talents,
your family. But allowing
Me to forgive others
through you—letting Me
be the Lord of your hurt, too.

I think I'm getting it, God.
But I still don't think it's fair.
I mean, she *did* hurt me!

Forgiveness isn't
always fair, My child.
But it's always right.

And sometimes it hurts
to do the right thing.

You *are* getting it!

Well, to be honest . . .
I *am* pretty tired of
carrying this grudge around.
I really miss my friendship
with Alison. I think I'll
go call her. I'm gonna need a
ride to youth group tonight.

And you're also going to
need a ride for Saturday.

Saturday?

That barbecue.
The cook-out at church.

Nah. I don't think
I wanna go. I'd be too
uncomfortable around Justin.

First dates usually
are a little uncomfortable.

First dates?

Justin.

You mean—

Yes.

Oh, my goodness!
I'd better run to the mall.
I don't have anything to wear!
I've gotta get moving!
I'll buy those khaki's I saw
marked down half-price,
and I might be able to get—

I wouldn't go just yet.

Why not?

Because before you'll even
have time to get to the mall,
your phone will be ringing.

Justin?!?! How do You know?
I mean, how can You—

Trust Me. I'm God.

You're right. I'll sit right here, God.
I'll stay right next to the phone,
and I won't pick it up until he calls.

No. Go ahead and
pick it up. There's
someone you need to call,
remember? She needs
your forgiveness.

Oh, yeah. And maybe
there's something else
I should give her.

Yes?

A huge apology.

You really are getting it, aren't you?

Well . . . I do have
a great Teacher.

I love you, My child.

Thanks. And God?

Yes?

Thanks, too, for
being patient enough
to keep on with me
until I finally get it.

"GREATER LOVE has
no one than this, that one lay
down his life for his FRIENDS."
(John 15:13)

Dear Susie:

My friend has confided something really personal to me: She's fascinated-with having sex. She says she knows what she's doing is wrong, but every time she gets into a dating situation with a guy, she just can't resist. She says she regrets it and tries to say no, but she always ends up giving in. I prayed with her, and she asked God to forgive her, but she always ends up falling back into her old routine. How can I help her resist this temptation?

April

Dear April:

I appreciate your deep concern for your friend. You asked how to help her resist temptation. Accountability will certainly help, but the Holy Spirit is the One who empowers us to say no.

I'm wondering if your friend was sexually abused in her younger years. Many times, girls who have that history, find it hard to say no in dating relationships. If she shares that with you, please encourage her to seek counseling. She may be equating sex with love.

I'm going to answer your the rest of your question as if you're the friend you wrote about, okay? Then, hopefully, you can take what I've shared with you and pass it on.

You may already know this, but let me remind you anyway: The blood of Christ is more than enough to cleanse you from every sin and mistake. When you surrender your life to Jesus, God makes you completely pure and spotless. "Therefore, if anyone is in Christ, he is a new creation; the old has gone, the new has come!" (2 Corinthians 5:17) And check out what 1 John 1:9 says: "If we confess our sins, he is faithful and just and will forgive us our sins and purify us from all unrighteousness."

Even though His forgiveness is exciting, it's not a free ticket to deliberately continue sinning (see Romans 6:1-2). True repentance means an attitude change that eventually shows up in your lifestyle. In other words, it means, "I don't intend to do that ever again!"

This doesn't mean you'll never be tempted again. You may always be tempted in the area of sexual activity. But that doesn't mean you have to give in. You see, this is where the Holy Spirit comes in. Once we decide to live in radical obedience to the lordship of Jesus Christ—totally surrendered to His will and not our own—we don't control our lives any longer. We give up control to God.

Galatians 2:20 talks about dying with Christ. In other words, we decide to give up our rights, our wants, our plans—just as Jesus did—to follow God's way. If you continue to give in to sexual

True repentance means an attitude change that eventually show up in your lifestyle.

temptation, you're not allowing God to have ownership of your life.

Check this out: "No temptation has seized you except what is common to man. And God is faithful; he will not let you be tempted beyond what you can bear" (1 Corinthians 10:13).

Here's another great verse to grab hold of: "Because he himself suffered when he was tempted, he is able to help those who are being tempted" (Hebrews 2:18).

Please find some good Christian friends, or an adult you trust, who can remind you of Scriptures like these when times get tough.

One more thing: Premarital sex *does* leave emotional scars in your life. This doesn't mean that you'll never have a good relationship with the opposite sex, but you definitely need to establish some accountability and strong boundaries in your life.

Sex is an incredible gift from God himself. I encourage you to claim secondary virginity and to remain sexually pure from now until you share wedding vows with a godly man for a lifetime of Christ-centered marriage.

Dear Susie:

I'm 16 years old, and I've never had a date. The problem is I want to, I'm scared I'll never marry, or no one will ever like me. It's kind of embarrassing. Some of my friends are two or three years younger and have already had many boyfriends. I just want one—someone really special. I'm not shy or quiet, and I have lots of friends that are guys, too. Help!

Brandi

Dear Brandi:

Even though this book is about helping your friends, I'm including your letter in here, because I know several girls reading this have a friend who feels exactly the same way you do.

I know it's tough that your younger friends have already had many boyfriends, but what does that prove? Only that they've had their heart broken and have had to deal with the frustration of rejection, and you haven't!

I get lots of mail from girls your age who think there must be something wrong with them simply because they don't have a boyfriend yet. What's the hurry? If everyone else put dirty socks on a chain and started wearing them around their neck, would you? I hope not!

Brandi, I wish you were here right now. I'd love to treat you to some ice cream and give you a big hug. Know what I'd tell you? "You're completely normal!"

Repeat after me: "I'm completely normal!" Say it again: "I'm completely normal!"

Brandi, many girls don't date until college, and other girls don't have a boyfriend until they're out of college and into a career. Please realize it's not a *guy* that gives meaning to your life—that can come only from a solid, growing relationship with your Creator.

It's totally normal to want a relationship with a guy. God created that desire within you. But His perfect timing. He's never early, yet He's never late.

Can I challenge you to do something? Will you memorize this verse? I'm going to give it to you from the Living Bible, because I like the way this particular version states it. Here it is:

> "But these things I plan won't happen right away. Slowly, steadily, surely, the time approaches when the vision will be fulfilled. If it seems slow, do not despair, for these things will surely come to pass. Just be patient! They will not be overdue a single day!"
>
> (Habakkuk 2:3)

Hey, Brandi, there *are* a few advantages of not being tied down to having a boyfriend right now. Don't believe me? Okay, I'll give you 99. You've gotta come up with the 100th-one on your own, okay? Here goes:

1. When you're ready for a new 'do, you don't have to worry about cutting off too much hair. (Why do guys like long hair anyway?)

2. You're more open to trying new things when you're flying solo. Try guitar lessons, sign up for a pottery class, join a Bible study.

3. There's more time for others when you're not sold out on one guy. Hang out with your family, visit people in nursing homes, shovel now off your neighbor's driveway.

4. You can eat an artichoke and onion pizza and not have to worry about impressing anyone with your breath.

5. Concentration exists. Your mind is completely clued in to your homework, your weekend job, your chores and most important (drum roll, please)— your relationship with God!

6. You can wear your favorite pair of platforms as much as you want! Who cares if you're taller than all the guys in your class?

7. When you're not in Coupleville, it's easier to avoid stuff God would never be too thrilled with—like feelings of jealousy and lust.

8. You can rent chick flicks as often as you want.

9. No worrying about what to give him on his birthday, Christmas and anniversaries.

10. No worrying about whether his buds like you.

11. No worrying about whether his parents like you.

12. Basically, just fewer worries.

13. God's timing is always perfect. It really, truly is! And if you need proof, check out Habakkuk 2:3.

14. If you ever held back in Foosball, Ping-Pong or pool just to make a guy feel good, you don't have to any more. Let your full potential soar!

15. There's more time to take a jog, hit the gym or walk your dog around the block.

16. Got a zit on your forehead? Who cares?

17. You've got lots more opportunities to hang out with the ultimate guy in your life—Jesus!

18. No special boy means no special break-ups. You get to avoid the crazy roller coaster so many others have gotten a bit queasy on.

[Got a zit on your forehead? Who cares?]

19. Everybody knows you as you, not so-and-so's other half.

20. When you're happy being single, you're able to set high standards for the kind of guy you'd like to go out with someday.

21. You can cry without being accused of PMS.

22. You don't have to have "the talk" about where your relationship is heading.

23. Building lots of good relationships with girls and guys is way more healthy than spending every waking second with one particular person.

24. No more sitting by the phone. You've got better things to do with your time.

25. Your room's a lot less cluttered. There just aren't as many things to save when a guy's not around.

26. You're into the courtship thing.

27. Hitting the mall with your girlfriends is tons better than with a guy 'cause they're more likely to understand why it takes you forever to decide between lilac and sky blue nail polish.

28. You can let your creative juices flow and put together a totally outrageous outfit without having to wonder what he'll think about it.

29. Telling the truth is much easier. Without a guy you'll never hear yourself say anything like, "Yeah, I love monster trucks," "I'd love to go hunting with you this weekend," or "Sure, the corner convenience store sounds like a great place to eat."

30. You've got your whole life ahead of you. Why rush into things? Just 'cause every other girl you know has a boyfriend? Come on! Who really wants to be just like everybody else, anyway?

31. The dough you would have spent on little gifts for him an go toward something more important—such as little gifts for your sponsored child in Ethiopia.

32. Maybe your parents have said, "No boyfriends for you, young lady." If so, no problem. Obedience is a good thing!

33. You know, sometimes boys have a not-so-great smell.

34. You've always loved fairy tales, nursery rhymes and limericks? Now you can write your own children's book! What are you waiting for? Get cranking!

35. The Diet Coke is all yours now. (And his backwash in long gone.)

36. You have plenty of opportunities to catch up on some bonding time with your mom or sister or long-lost friend from camp.

37. No gal-pals from his past to deal with.

38. Rebecca St. James, Margaret Becker, Jaci Velasquez, Kathy Troccoli—all single women fulfilled in their relationship with Christ. If they can be secure without a guy, you can too!

39. Your friends don't get antsy when you're taking a long time to get ready for an evening of fun.

40. Instead of listening to his band play at the local coffee shop, you and the girls can start your own band!

41. No more badgering your friends to find out if they really like him!

42. You finally have a chance to fill your diary with stuff other than him—you know, dreams, goals, answers to prayer.

43. You can spend Friday evening with a bowl of popcorn, a bottle of Snapple and *The Princess Bride* and not have to worry about him being bored.

44. No more looking at *Field and Stream* magazine—unless you really want to.

45. Bored without a boyfriend? No need to be! Try creating your own board game. Hey, it was probably a woman without a guy who created "Candy Land" and "Sorry!"

46. It's way cool to be able to check the oil in your car all by yourself.

47. You now have some spare moments to pull out the sewing machine and make that too-cool skirt and top you've had your eye on.

48. Hey, you could even design your own pattern!

49. No more straining to read between the lines to figure out what he's really saying.

50. Finally! You've got an opportunity to really get involved in church. Consider helping out in the nursery, teaching the kindergarten Sunday school class or visiting a senior citizen who hasn't been able to attend in a while.

51. You get to spend Monday nights watching "7th Heaven."

52. Every single day of spring break can be spent with the girls, and you don't have to feel guilty about leaving him out.

53. No stressing about where things to after high school. You can confidently head off to the college of your choice!

54. When you hear a girl in the hallway talking about her disastrous relationship, you can lend a caring

ear and feel grateful that you're not in her situation.

55. No need to revolve your summer plans around him—God's got big plans for you! Hey, maybe you'll head overseas on a life-changing missions adventure!

56. Don't wanna wash your hair today? Then don't!

57. No need to explain why a brownie topped with chocolate ice cream, doused in chocolate chips and hot fudge served with a cup of hot chocolate is a great lunch.

58. You can listen to all your fave girl bands without having to switch to his music picks.

59. You're not spending time with someone simply because you feel guilty about saying no to his relentless offers to take you out to dinner.

60. Yahoo! You can hum the tune that keeps floating around in your head without feeling self-conscious.

61. You don't have to rack your brain trying to come up with a bunch of conversation starters to get him talking.

62. And those long awkward silences are now a thing of the past. (Maybe only a temporary thing of the past, but still, be glad that you're not having to work your way around them at this point in time!)

63. You can throw yourself into doing more around the house. Why not gather up all the stuff no one uses anymore and have a giant garage sale? Then use the moolah to do something nice for someone else.

64. When you ace trig, make the honor roll and start on the girls' varsity b-ball team, there's no wonder-

ing whether he's intimidated by your accomplishments.

65. You can finish your steak and eat your loaded baked potato without worrying if you-know-who thinks you're eating too much.

66. Now that your mind's not all caught up in coupledom, you can play around in the kitchen with your friends. Why not create your own brand-new recipe for mouthwatering chocolate chip cookies?

67. When you're having major cramps, you can go ahead and scream or withdraw and not make excuses.

68. Think of the variety of photographs you can surround yourself with! Life's kinda boring when you've got the same face staring at you from your dresser, your bedside table, your closet door and your bathroom mirror.

69. You can wear your favorite navy sweater two Friday nights in a row without having a guy say, "Hey, isn't that what you wore last weekend?"

70. There are more available hours for you to spend baby-sitting, which means you'll have more money of your own—to put toward your car, your college education or your summer missions trip.

71. Have you been to the library lately? There are rows and rows of books there that'll pique your interest and send your mind and imagination into the lives of people from past and present. Find out more about other cool single women such as Amy Carmichael and Corrie ten Boom.

72. There's no need to leave your house any sooner than necessary to get to school or youth group. You don't have to pick up any carless boys.

73. Your cat's a lot happier now that no one's picking it up by its tail.

74. Church, school, hockey games, dc Talk concerts, thrift stores . . . at this point in life, who really has time for one guy?

75. You're free to wear the jacket of your choice without feeling like you should be wearing his.

76. The fridge and cupboards at your house are more likely to stay well-stocked since they aren't raided every day after school by someone who could eat you out of house and home.

77. You have absolute, total control of the TV remote!

78. Goodbye to being grilled by friends, parents, youth workers, etc. about every second you spent with a certain XY-chromosomed person.

79. When you're at a school activity, you're completely free to hang with more than one guy.

80. You've got more room in your locker than either of the attached girls with lockers next to yours.

81. There are enough things in life to say no to without having to deal with a guy who's pressuring you to get a little more personal than you want.

82. You have to bother with makeup only when you really want to.

83. You've been wanting to redecorate your room? Now's your chance.

84. You can start your Christmas shopping early! Hey, in one month all the winter stuff will be 60 percent off!

85. Without anyone asking you out, there's no chance to being stood up.

86. Your girlfriends will probably like you more now. This is a good time to maintain the friendships you might be ignoring if you had a steady guy.

87. No more having to share half of your Twix. You can eat both candy bars yourself. (Two for me. None for you.)

88. You don't have to deal with someone who's jealous when you're friendly with other guys.

89. Remember how your dad insisted that your last guy take his baseball cap off at the dinner table? You can certainly do without going through that again!

90. You'll probably have fewer all-around mortifying moments since you're not spending time with someone you really want to impress.

91. It's highly possible that you'll get more out of your youth group if you're not attached at the hip to a significant other. You'll probably hang with more people and focus better on your youth pastor's talks.

92. You can finally check out that part-time job you've been dying to get.

93. Have you always wanted to try your hand at watercolor? Get out the paints and go for it!

You don't have to deal with someone who's jealous when you're friendly with other guys.

94. Now you have time to memorize 2
Corinthians
4:7-9.

95. After you've memorized the above
Scripture, you've got time to get some
adhesive paper and create your own
bumper sticker based on this verse.

96. When something cracks you up, like a
great joke or a hilarious movie scene, you
can laugh so hard that you snort and not
have to be embarrassed about it.

97. Tired of the same ol' same ol' TV sitcoms?
Why not create your own?

98. You won't have to hear your friends say, "Are
you talking about him again?"

99. Nothing's more attractive than a confident
single gal who truly loves Jesus and feels secure
in who He's created her to be.

Okay, now it's your turn. Think of one more
reason, and jot it here in the space provided. And again, don't be
fooled into thinking that having a boyfriend will validate you.
Only God can do that.

100.

> "The purposes of a man's heart are deep waters, but a man of UNDERSTANDING draws them out."
>
> (Proverbs 20:5)

Dear Susie:

I have a Christian friend who uses hell as a swear word when she's not around her parents. She sees nothing wrong with it. I'm pretty sure it's wrong, but I don't know how to explain it.

Lindsey

Dear Lindsey:

Not only does Solomon warn us about swearing in Proverbs 4:24: "Put away perversity from your mouth; keep corrupt talk far from your lips," but Paul also comes out strongly against it in Ephesians 4:29-32: "Do not let any unwholesome talk come out of your mouths, but only what is helpful for building others up according to their needs, that it may benefit those who listen. And do not grieve the Holy Spirit of God, with whom you were sealed for the day of redemption. Get rid of all bitterness, rage and anger, brawling and slander, along with every form of malice. Be kind and compassionate to one another, forgiving each other just as in Christ God forgave you."

And then again in Ephesians 5:4. "Nor should there be obscenity, foolish talk or coarse joking, which are out of place."

It was wrong then, and it's wrong now. It concerns me that your friend calls herself a Christian and continues to cuss. A Christian should live as Christ lives. What kind of witness is she setting for nonbelievers? People who aren't Christians want to see the *difference* in our lives—not how much we have in common.

Please share these Scriptures with her and ask if she'd *like* to quit swearing. It may be that she *wants* to stop, but has simply gotten into a bad habit that's now hard to break.

Is there something you'd like to give up in your life? Maybe too many Cokes, too much TV, etc. Ask if the two of you can hold each other accountable to stopping a habit that you'd like to get rid of. You ask her if she's used inappropriate language today, and she'll ask you if you've . . . (whatever you decide you're going to give up).

And if she *doesn't* want to stop cursing? Gently call her on it. Ask how she can maintain an intimate, growing relationship with Christ and continue to go directly against God's command.

Dear Susie:

My best friend told me that I'm a mooch. I don't think I am. I really want to be a great friend. What do you think?

Hillary

Dear Hillary:

Since I don't know you personally, I can't make that call. But if she's really your best friend, I'm guessing she's probably trying to help you. Sometimes it's tough to tell our friends what they need to hear.

Examine yourself. *Are* you a mooch? Do you borrow a lot of things from several different people and take your time returning those items?

Maybe this will help you determine if your friend is on track or not:

Who, Me–a Mooch?

Find out if you'r the one who always wants a handout!

by Anne Williman

Constantly borrowing things from friends and family without paying them back? You may be a mooch! You know, someone who freeloads off others so much that everyone grimaces when she appears. Take this quiz to see if you qualify as mooch material.

1. The afternoon of the bowling party, all your favorite shirts are in the dirty clothes hamper. Your sister's got a new WWJD T-shirt, but she's at work. You

   a. call her at her job, begging to borrow it. If she says forget it, you dig out the Audio Adrenaline shirt you wore only half a day last Thursday.

   b. take her T-shirt. She probably won't notice it's gone. If she does, you'll make it up to her sometime in the next decade.

   c. ask your mother if it's cool for you to wear your sister's shirt. Then if you sister has a problem with it, she can take it up with Mom.

2. While at a Chinese restaurant with your friend, you have only enough cash to pay for the sweet and sour chicken dish that you absolutely love. But an egg roll sounds great, too. You

a. plead with your friend to spring for an egg roll. What's a couple of bucks between best friends?

b. promise to invite your friend to dinner the next time your older brother's home from college. The only cost to her? One egg roll.

c. choose a cheaper dinner so you can squeeze out enough for the tasty egg roll.

3. Your friend wants her new dc Talk CD back, but you're not sure where you stashed it. You

a. destroy your room as you look for it. If unsuccessful, you forfeit the water park outing with your youth group and use the money to replace your friend's CD.

b. get an unlisted phone number and start wearing a wig to school. That way your now ex-friend will never find you.

c. level with your friend about the CD being lost. But you tell her when it turns up, she'll get it pronto. Meanwhile, you let her borrow your Supertones CD.

4. At the open house of the new crisis pregnancy center, a bucket is passed for donations. You

a. take a long drink of punch just as it comes your way—hoping it'll be passed around you.

b. dig out a couple of bucks from your jeans pocket. You were going to use the cash to repay Dad for yesterday's loan at Dairy Queen, but he'd support this cause, and you can repay him anytime.

c. pass the bucket without making a contribution, but ask for an envelope with the center's address on it. After you baby-sit next weekend, you can send a gift.

5. To prepare for the Solo and Ensemble Contest, you need private flute lessons. A woman at church offers to give you lessons if you'll help her out by watching her kids. You

a. talk with your mom about a fair exchange rate for her lessons and your baby-sitting. Then you keep careful records of when and how long the two of you swapped services.

b. decide to take her offer and show up for all of your flute lessons, but flake out a few times when she needs a sitter.

c. present your dad with his favorite candy bar, and then

beg him to finance the lessons so you won't have to baby-sit.

6. Mom's 14-karat gold chain looks perfect with the mauve sweater you're wearing to the movies. You decide to borrow the chain. Once you're in the theater, you notice it's broken and fallen into your lap. You
   a. jet out of the theater and hit the nearest discount store for a cheap imitation. Your mother will never know the difference.
   b. call your older brother and ask if he'll take you to get it fixed. He'll have to spring for the cost of the repair, but you'll promise to do his chores for the next six months.
   c. plan to tell your mom how sorry you are and offer to save your money to pay for the repair.

7. Some girls from church are planning to buy a birthday present for your friend Angie. "Chip in any amount," they tell you. "Most people give about $5." You
   a. for over five bucks and offer to wrap the gift after it's been purchased.
   b. plead with the friend next to you to drop in a dollar on your behalf since you left your purse at home. You promise to repay her as soon as you can, which may be a while since you're low on cash.
   c. remember that Angie didn't get you anything last Christmas and decide to throw in a couple of dollars for her gift.

8. Your Sunday school class is having a potluck after church tomorrow. You
   a. beg Mom to bake her delicious three-layer chocolate brownies. She doesn't have much to do today, and you're going to the mall with friends.
   b. grab a bag of generic BB! potato chips on the way to church. Hey, they said to bring one dish, and those chips will fill a bowl. (Okay, maybe a small one!)
   c. slip Mom a five to buy ingredients for taco salad at the grocery store. Once she's home with the goods, you get started on your creation for the potluck.

SCORING:

1. a=2, b=0, 3=1
2. a=0, b=1, c=2
3. a=2, b=0, c=1
4. a=0, b=1, c=2
5. a=2, b=0. c=1
6. a=0, b=1, c=2
7. a=2, b=0. c=1
8. a=0, b=1, c=2

Add up your points.

12-16 points: Congrats! Mooching isn't a significant problem for you. You appreciate it when someone does something for you, and you make every effort to pay him or her back.

8-11 points: You tend to expect others to do for you without having to give them anything in return. Before you alienate friends or family members with this kind of attitude, ask God to help you become more sensitive about when you're mooching. Then work to improve.

Below 8 points: You *do* have room for improvement! But don't fret! The Lord can help you turn around and become more focused on meeting others' needs. Ask Him to help you identify when and from whom you mooch. When you blow it with someone, apologize and do something nice for him or her. It'll take some work on your part, but pretty soon you'll see people smile when you enter the room!

"A GENTLE ANSWER turns away wrath, but a HARSH WORD stirs up anger."
(Proverbs 15:1)

Dear Susie:

This is my first year in public school, so I was glad to find a morning prayer group. But there were some things about Chase—our student leader—that made me uncomfortable. He was always hugging us and telling everyone how God had ordained him to preach.

Then I found out that Chase is bisexual. And no, it's not a rumor. I left the prayer group. Some of my friends still go, and I don't know how to tell them about Chase without gossiping.

I don't know him well enough to confront him about it, even though the Bible says to confront a brother one-on-one if he's in sin.

In a school where Christians are already viewed critically, I think some kids think being gay is okay now. After all Chase is gay, and he's the leader of the prayer group. What should I do?

Katrina

Dear Katrina:

I'm sorry this has happened, and I can understand why you feel uncomfortable. I encourage you to first of all, turn to Lord in prayer. He cares about every single detail of your life, and this situation is certainly no exception. You can tell God everything that you're thinking and feeling, and then trust Him to work things out in His time and in His way.

Sounds like Chase is very confused. We have a "Gender Specialists" department here at Focus on the Family who minister to thousands of teenagers and young adults who are deceived into believing they're gay or bisexual. The folks who head up this great department are men who have come out of the gay lifestyle, and they'll all tell you that the homosexual lifestyle is a lie from Satan.

Most gay men did not have a good, strong, godly relationship with their father. Every boy needs the love of a godly man. When he doesn't get it, he feels a void in his life. Many times without realizing it, he'll seek the attention and physical closeness from another male and automatically assume he must be gay.

Who's the father of lies? Satan. Who's the Author of Peace? Jesus Christ. Satan would love to continue deceiving Chase and cause him to doubt his masculinity. Satan is using a void in Chase's life to confuse him about his sexuality.

Of course, you can't tell Chase that. You've already said that you don't know him well enough to confront him. But you *can* continue to be kind to him. Smile and say hi to him when you pass him in the hall.

Maybe you can tell him privately that you appreciate his leadership skills in the Bible club, but you're not comfortable with his lifestyle and the fact that he's condoning it to others. Let him know you'll continue praying for the group, but you'll be watching only from a distance. That way, he won't wonder why you've suddenly dropped out.

Will you also consider sharing this with your parents and another Christian adult you trust—such as your youth leader, Sunday school teacher or pastor? One reason God has put these people into your life is to help you with situations like the one you're facing. They may have had similar experiences when they were your age. They may also have some valuable insight to share, and they could pray with you about this, too.

Dear Susie:

I'm really worried about my friend, Ryan. He only wears black clothing and he's totally into the gothic scene. I realize that it's not a sin to wear a specific color, but there's something different about him. He's not his old self. He's getting weird. I don't understand this whole goth thing at all, and I'm scared for him.

Samantha

Dear Samantha:

You're right—it's not a sin to wear the color black, but it sounds like Ryan is into more than simply color-coordinating his wardrobe.

There's a college student at my church who used to be in the goth movement. I've asked him to share his story in order to help you understand the movement a little better.

From Gothic To Godly

Ever wonder if you can fill life's void with something other than God? Here's one guy who tried. And failed.

When 15-year-old Erin Crow let junior high and headed to high school, he struggled with the transition. With extra time on his hands during the summer, he became a big fan on the movie *The Crow*. He also found new musical interest in Nine Inch Nails.

"I bought every single one of their albums," Erin says. "Trent Reznor became my idol. It was like I began turning into a Nine-Inch Nails and Crow disciple. I was very insecure and didn't like myself at all.

Through His Ears to His Face

It didn't take too long before Erin decided that simply listening to the music wasn't enough. He began to dress in an all-black gothic style and wear makeup.

"I used basic white on my face to make myself look really pale," Erin says. "I wanted to look sick and deathly. Then I'd use black to outline my eyes and lips and paint my thumbnails and pinkie nails black.

"I became obsessed with death," he continues, "and I wouldn't wear anything but black. I grew my hair really long and even dyed it black to be like The Crow."

Erin began making daily trips to the cemetery and taking naps among the tombstones. He eventually got into vampiric stuff, but still felt a huge emptiness inside his heart.

"I didn't like myself," he says. "I was trying to become a different person—trying to find fulfillment. I even became sexually involved with my girlfriend." When he was 18, Erin moved with his girlfriend from Colorado to Tennessee to live together near her family. "But you know what? I still wasn't whole. Something was missing," he says.

And Then it Happened

"One day while on a farm in Tennessee, I was swinging an aluminum baseball bat against a tree," Erin says. "It ricocheted back and hit my cheekbone, splitting my skin and cracking my tooth. I immediately dropped to my knees and began praying. 'I need Your help, Jesus,' I said. I was scared and knew the Lord had been trying to get my attention."

Erin says God used that experience to wake him up spiritually. He witnessed to his girlfriend, but she wouldn't listen. Even though it meant leaving his girlfriend behind in Tennessee, he called his mom and explained that he wanted to come home. She sent him an airline ticket, and he was soon back in Colorado.

New Life

"When I came home," he says, "God started changing my life. I lost my obsession with sex and cemeteries and wearing all-black clothing and makeup. The music didn't even interest me anymore. It's like I started seeing it through God's eyes, and it all began to disgust me."

As Erin gave control of his life to Jesus Christ, he also began to see *himself* in a new light. "I now like who I am," he says. "I'm a child of God, Erin Crow, not a Nine-Inch-Nails wannabe. I've been made in God's image."

And has that changed his dating habits? "I've asked God to forgive me for being sexually active outside of marriage," Erin says. "I'm so grateful He not only forgives me but also gives me a brand-new start. I'm claiming spiritual virginity. I know that physically I can't undo what I'd done, but I can commit to sexual purity and remain a spiritual virgin until I get married. I'm determined not to go beyond hand-holding and maybe a hug with any girl I date. In fact, I've decided not to even kiss a girl until I'm married to her."

Erin says that his former girlfriend got her own wake-up call about a year after he left Tennessee. She was badly injured in a car wreck and gave her life to Christ while recovering in the hospital. Today she's a committed Christian, too.

But What About . . .

Can't someone just dress gothic and not really get messed up?

"There's a lot of New Age stuff mixed in with the whole gothic culture," Erin says. "In fact, if you go back far enough, you'll find there are actually satanic roots in this movement. Witchcraft is also prevalent in gothic culture.

"When someone simply dresses the part, it's called kindergarten gothic. But here's the danger: When you step into something, you always get more involved in it if you're actually doing it day by day. True gothic is a lifestyle. It changes the way you live and talk—everything!"

And for the teen who says, "I just want to be different!"?

"It's a downward spiral," Erin warns. "It doesn't take long for Satan to get such a grasp on your life that you don't know what to do. I mean, I was contemplating suicide. For the teen who says, 'I just wanna wear the clothes and do the makeup,' he's kidding himself. It's a lie. Satan will use it to damage him."

"Take note of this: EVERYONE should be quick to LISTEN, slow to speak and slow to become angry."
(James 1:19)

Final Thoughts

Erin's favorite verse is John 10:10: "The thief comes only to steal and kill and destroy; I have come that they may have life, and have it to the full."

"That's what happens through the gothic culture," he says. "Satan uses it to destroy you and to steal your identity."

Erin is now plugged into church and is attending a Christian college. "I really have to watch the music I listen to. It has a big effect on me. I pretty much limit my music to Christian stuff," he says.

Even though God has forgiven him, Erin still faces the consequences of sin. "I struggle with thoughts about my past," he says. "I'm continually giving it to God over and over again. I want Him to consistently be Lord of my life. I sometimes struggle with truly praising God and forgetting who's around me. I don't want other people's opinions to hold me back from worship."

Erin's advice to teens who want to deepen their relationship with Christ? "Don't settle for simply reading the Bible—study it. Since Jesus has completely changed my life and truly set me free, I now have an intense desire to win people to the Lord. He's given me such a hunger for His Word. I want to know it well enough to give answers to those who believe false teachings."

I hope you'll feel comfortable enough to share Erin's story with your friend Ryan. Don't stop hanging around him simply because he's frightening you. Assure him there's nothing he can wear that will cause you to stop being his friend. At the same time, though, let him know you're uncomfortable with the changes you see happening in his life.

Dear Susie:

I hear a lot about the "Last Days" and Christians being persecuted in other countries, but I've never thought a lot about it. I have a friend, though, who is really frightened about all this. She says she's afraid God is going to ask her to go through persecution some day. She's a strong Christian, and I admire her relationship with the Lord. But it's weird hearing her say this stuff. It makes me uncomfortable.

Sarah

Dear Sarah:

The Bible *does* say that in the last days Christians will be persecuted for their faith. Many people believe we're in the last days right now. Christians in Sudan, Africa and other parts of the world are definitely under persecution. In some countries, Christians can be killed for even meeting together. In Sudan, if your Christianity is discovered, you can be thrown in a refugee camp, beaten and tortured, and your children can be sold as slaves.

We have it a lot easier in North America, don't we? Still, I get letters from teen girls who are made fun of at school, home or at their part-time jobs because of their faith in Christ.

No one can say whether your friend really *will* be persecuted for her religious beliefs. It could be that she's simply frightened because of all that she's seen on the news. But it could also be that God is preparing her heart and mind for something that you and I don't know about.

Remember the violent killing spree at Columbine High School in Littleton, Colorado? Seventeen-year-old Cassie Bernall was certainly persecuted for her faith.

It's been awhile since that's been on the news. Let me refresh your memory, with an article we printed in *Brio* magazine, okay?

> But it could also be that God is preparing her heart and mind for something that you and I don't know about.

Remembering Columbine
by Marty McCormack

Jesus said, "I am the gate; whoever enters through me will be saved. He will come in and go out, and find pasture. The thief comes only to steal and kill and destroy; I have come that they may have life, and have it to the full" (John 10:9-10).

One by one, we're all going to stand before the gate. Those who proclaim Jesus as their Savior will know the gate and enter through Him to find eternal life. Others who choose an alternate way will be on a path that only leads to death.

The 12 students and one teacher who were killed at Columbine High School in Littleton, Colo., stood before that gate. They didn't know their turn to die would come so soon, but there was little they could do to prevent it. All they *could* do was be prepared.

Of the Christians who entered through the gate on April 20, 1999, 17-year-old Cassie Bernall was a current *Brio* reader, and 17-year-old Rachel Scott was a former *Brio* reader.

Cassie Bernall

The story of Cassie's life and death has made its way around the globe, and the last moments of her life have become a testimony to all who have heard of her boldness. She's been called a martyr because she was killed immediately after declaring her faith in God. But Cassie was more than a martyr. She was a daughter, a sister, a friend, a student and a child of God.

"There was a quiet side to Cassie, but also a real fun-loving side," says her pastor, George Kirsten of West Bowles Community Church. "She had a name for different people. I think she called my 13-year-old son, who's kind of gregarious, a tree frog or tree monkey. Cassie was also a thinker. She liked to get in to deeper conversations, and she talked a lot about her walk with Christ—not only with the kids at church, but also with the kids at school."

Cassie made it a priority to be involved with her youth group and spent Tuesday evenings meeting with a discipleship group. The group was going through a book called *Seeking Peace.* She had been underlining important points in the book and making side notes of personal applications. Pastor Kirsten explains that Cassie's brother, Chris, found the following note in her room on Tuesday night, when it became clear that she wouldn't be coming home. Cassie wrote this on the day she died:

"Now I have given up on everything else. I have found it to be the only way to really know Christ, and to experience the mighty power that brought Him back to life again, and to find out what it means to suffer and to die with Him. So, whatever it takes, I will be one who lives in the fresh newness of life of those who are alive with the dead."

Seventeen-year-old Crystal Woodman, a friend of

But Cassie was more than a martyr. She was a daughter, a sister, a friend, a student and a child of God.

Cassie's, says Cassie truly lived out her faith and was always finding ways to serve. She remembers how Cassie loved greeting first-time visitors to their youth group and how she enjoyed volunteering with an inner-city ministry called Victory Outreach.

Pastor Kirsten knows of Cassie's involvement with Victory Outreach, too. "She'd go down there along with the youth group and hang out with a pretty rough bunch," he says. "She'd talk to prostitutes, gang members and people just out of prison about the Lord. She was increasingly bold."

Crystal, who was one student spared from the bullets flying through Columbine's library, says, "Cassie loved photography and was really good at it. She liked to snowboard and hike and liked animals."

And above all else, Cassie cared about people. Crystal says Cassie had talked about her hopes to work in the medical field someday. "I know she was planning on volunteering at a hospital this summer," Crystal says. "And then she was going to cut off her hair for the chemo patients. It was amazing. She was constantly trying to help people."

With these few examples, it's easy to see that Cassie took on a sincere love for people since giving her life to Christ two years ago. "Cassie was a light for Christ," says 17-year-old Craig Moon, a close friend of Cassie's.

Crystal agrees. "She died for her faith. That's why she died and that's how she lived her whole life. She was a martyr for Jesus."

Cassie's parents, Brad and Misty Bernall, have this statement to share: "Our daughter, Cassie, was no saint. She was far from perfect, but she was prepared. Her final word, 'Yes,' will always be a challenge and inspiration to us. Our prayer is that her 'Yes' will be proclaimed aloud by many more to come. Cassie, as one of her friends expressed, has raised the bar for all of us. Let us be determined to see that it is never lowered."

"My GRACE is sufficient for you, for my POWER is made PERFECT in WEAKNESS." —Jesus Christ."

(2 Corinthians 12:9)

Rachel Scott

Always taking opportunities to tell others about her faith in Christ, Rachel Scott often used her talents in the arts for God's glory. She acted in school plays and choreographed productions to Christian music for class assignments. One of her favorites was a mime to the Ray Boltz song "Watch the Lamb."

Rachel often expressed herself through poetry, too, and wrote one poem that illustrates the significance of each person knowing Jesus as Savior. Inside a print of her hand, Rachel wrote:

"What if you were to die today? What would happen to you? Where would you go? Tomorrow is not a promise, but a chance. It may not be there for you. After death, then what? Where will you spend your eternity? Will you have an eternal life without your loving Father, or will you be ripped from the arms of your Savior, Jesus Christ? Eternity is in your hands . . . Change it!"

Rachel was near the end of her senior year of high school at the time of her death. She had dreamed of serving in Africa as a missionary. A co-worker and friend of Rachel's, Rob Salyer, told *The Washington Post*, "I think Rachel thought of Africa because there's so much suffering there. She wanted to help relieve the suffering."

Student Sarah Arzola has a necklace with half a charm that says, "Best Friends for Life."

"Rachel has the other one," Sarah said as she spoke with *The Denver Rocky Mountain News*. "We were complete opposites, but we were best friends."

Soon after Rachel's death, her mother, Beth Nimmo, spoke with a reporter from the Christian Broadcasting Network. She said, "I'm so glad Rachel knew the Lord. It is a comfort to know that our relationship will be restored at some point. She was everything a mother could want, and I thank God for letting me have her and letting me love and take care of her as long as I did."

The Good in the Bad

Because of the way Cassie and Rachel lived, much was accomplished in their death. The Holy Spirit worked through the testimonies of two young girls to change eternity for many other people. God has advanced His kingdom in a visible way through the tragedy in Littleton. As Joseph said in the Old Testament, "You intended to harm me, but God meant it for good to accomplish what is now being done, the saving of many lives" (Genesis 50:20).

"Cassie was ready," Crystal says. "We all have to be ready like Cassie was—constantly reading the Word, constantly serving, constantly living our lives for Christ."

The gunman cornered Cassie in the school library, pointed his gun in her face and screamed, "Do you believe in God?" Without hesitation, Cassie quickly responded, "YES! I believe!" And with that, she was killed.

I don't know if your friend will be cornered or persecuted for her faith, but the important thing is that she be ready—that we *all* be ready. I realize it's not easy for you to hear her talk about the possibility of dying as a martyr, but listen to her feelings and continue encouraging her to share them with you.

Since you're both Christians, why not pray regularly together? None of us knows how long we have left on this earth. Make it a point to ask God to continually keep you standing strong for Him.

> Dear Susie:
> I've recently made a new friend, and she's really nice, but she doesn't know God. I don't know how to witness to her without sounding pushy.
> Kellie

Dear Kellie:
Unfortunately, many girls your age are so absorbed in their own struggles that they're unwilling or unable to reach out and minister to others. You're a bright exception, and I'm encouraged by your enthusiasm.

The Bible is very clear that Jesus wants *everyone* to be saved. "The Lord is not slow in keeping his promise, as some understand slowness. He is patient with you, not wanting anyone to perish, but everyone to come to repentance" (2 Peter 3:9).

It's comforting to know that Jesus wants your friend saved even more than you do! Love her unconditionally. Ask God to help you reflect His character. Talk about the Lord in a natural way—instead of preaching at her or "telling" her what she "should" know.

Have you ever given your personal testimony to someone? If not, now would be a great time to practice. Jot down what your life was like *before* you met Christ, how you came to know Him in His fullness and the difference He's making in your life today. Try to keep it under three minutes.

Also, consider inviting her to your youth group. Surrounding her with several Christian friends from church will help her see the difference in your life and the lives of nonbelievers at school.

If you'd like more tips on witnessing, grab a copy of a book I wrote with a friend of mine: *Keeping Your Cool While Sharing Your Faith.*

Dear Susie:

My good friend, Shelli, is kinda selfish. I mean, it feels like she's kind of a mooch sometimes. I've talked with my mom about it, and she says, "Keep being her friend, but let this make you aware of the kind of friend you don't want to be."

Abigail

Dear Abigail:

Your mom is right. We learn good *and* bad stuff from our friends. Your friend probably doesn't even realize how others are looking at her. Tell you what, I'll pop a quiz in here that you can nonchalantly show her and take together. It will also serve as a reminder to *you* not to become like her!

"A cheerful look brings JOY to the heart."
(Proverbs 15:30)

The Gift of Giving

Time to check up on your personal
pattern of giving and taking!

by Sarah Meekhof

Jesus Christ was the ultimate giver and taker. He gave of Himself—His time, His gifts and ultimately His life. Yet He also received from His Father spiritual strength, emotional comfort and eventually His life from death. Jesus was a dynamic giver and a gracious receiver.

What about *you*? Are you able to receive as well as you give, or do you find yourself taking advantage of the generosity of others? Take this quiz and find out just where you stand.

1. In your friendships, you find that you are the one who calls and keeps in contact.

5	4	3	2	1
Most often		It's even		Seldom

2. You think of thoughtful little things to do for other people.

5	4	3	2	1
Constantly		Sometimes		Not much

3. Your friends say that you're a good listener.

5	4	3	2	1
All the time		Often		Not ever

4. You're willing to be there when a friend needs something—even if it means sacrificing your time or your own plans.

5	4	3	2	1
Always		It depends		Not really

5. You allow friends to borrow clothes and money.

5	4	3	2	1
Whevever they need it		Not often		Never

Jesus was a dynamic giver and a gracious receiver.

6. Friends ask you to help them out with homework and projects.

5	4	3	2	1
Regularly		Now and then		Rarely

7. You have trouble saying no when someone asks for a favor.

5	4	3	2	1
That's me		Sort of		No

8. You find that 80 percent of your time is spent doing for others.

5	4	3	2	1
Yes		More like 40 percent		Zip, zero, nada

SCORING:

31-40 points: You're an extreme giver. Giving is great, but it *could* end up being too much of a good thing. Do people take advantage of you? Are you burned out? Remember that it's okay to be on the receiving end once in a while. You need both giving and receiving to have a healthy balance in your life.

21-30 points: You're doing well in both categories. Not only are you willing to sacrifice your time and talents, but you can graciously receive from others when the time is right. Keep up the good balance!

8-20 points: If you fall in this zone, you are definitely a *taker*. Receiving for you is a habit. That's okay—as long as the generosity of others isn't abused. You need to make an effort to reach out to others.

> "The tongue that brings HEALING
> is a tree of life, but a deceitful
> tongue crushes the spirit."
> (Proverbs 15:4)

Dear Susie:

I have many friends, but not one I can call a best friend. I don't know how long I can go without having a good Christian friend whom I can write to and talk with. Please help!

Megan

Dear Megan:

I'm glad you have several friends. A best friend is great, but not *essential* to your happiness. I'm guessing, from the sound of your letter, that you just don't have *Christian* friends. I admire you for wanting to establish a friendship with someone who shares your deepest belief in God.

Ask your mom to pray *with* you for God to raise up a Christian young lady at your school. It could be that there are several Christian students, but you're just not aware of it.

One way to find out who the Christians are is to participate at the annual "See You At The Pole" event every September. Christians all around the world meet at the flagpole of their schools on a specific day and pray for their school.

I'll give you the hotline number, so you can get more information, okay? **See You at the Pole, P.O. Box 60134, Fort Worth, TX 76115. 817-447-7526. www.syatp.com** Meanwhile, keep *being* a friend to those around you.

Dear Susie:

My best friend, Allison, is really scared about all the violence that's happening in schools today. I want to help her, but I'm not sure how. I'm a little scared, too, but not like Allison. She thinks about the possibility of getting shot at school almost every single day.

Kristi

Dear Kristi:

Unfortunately, many schools *have* become frightening environments because of all the shootings that have been happening. Fear is a normal human reaction, but God doesn't want us to *live* in fear. He is the Author of Peace, and he wants you and your friends to bask in that peace.

A friend of mine wrote an article that we printed in *Brio* magazine that covers this very subject. I'll pop it in right here, so you can show it to Allison, okay?

letters to
SUSIE **155**

You've Got What it Takes
No need to fear—Christ is here!
by Marty McCormack

With the start of another season that sends you off to public or private school, have you found yourself thinking that home schooling sounds better and better all the time? Even if you love to learn, love to see your friends everyday, love to stay after hours for sports practice or band rehearsal, you may be one of many with an uneasiness about just being *in* a school building.

So much violence has occurred in schools across the United States in recent years that young people from kindergarten to 12th grade are apprehensive about being in a classroom where evil seems to reign. But you know what? If you're a Christian, you have Christ and the Holy Spirit dwelling inside you. That means through Christ, you've got the power, you've got the strength, you've got what it takes to go to school without fear.

Check out these verses from the Bible:

- "I will remain in the world no longer, but they are still in the world, and I am coming to you. Holy Father, protect them by the **power** of your name—the name you gave me—so that they may be one as we are one" (John 17:11, emphasis added).

- "I thank Christ Jesus our Lord, who has given me **strength,** that he considered me faithful, appointment me to his service" (1 Timothy 1:12, emphasis added).

- "But even if you should suffer for what is right, you are blessed. **'Do not fear** what they fear; do not be frightened' " (1 Peter 3:14, emphasis added).

A Healthy Perspective

Bad things are going to happen; and Jesus tells us that we'll have trouble in this world (John 16:33). People are going to sin; God knows the state of our hearts (Genesis 8:21). Evil men will sometimes prosper; yet we serve a God who's in complete control of everything (Proverbs 11:21). Nothing escapes Him. Nothing surprises Him. He knows what's going to happen, and He knows how He's going to respond.

The question is, how do *you* respond when you see bad things happening, people sinning and evil progressing? Here are some courses of action to take you through the murky waters.

No. 1: Be Joyful, Pray and Give Thanks

God clearly spells out His will for us—the way He wants us to behave—in all situations: "Be joyful always; pray continually; give thanks in all circumstances, for this is God's will for you in Christ Jesus" (1 Thessalonians 5:16-18).

It's not easy to be joyful when everything around us looks gloomy. It's not easy pray when we don't understand what God's doing. It's not easy to give thanks when something's been done against us. But God tells us *it is His will* for us to be joyful, to pray and give thanks. When we allow the Holy Spirit to guide us in these things through the tough times, we'll be one step closer to responding to evil in a way that pleases God.

No. 2: Recall God's Promises

The Bible records many promises God has given us. Take time to study the Word daily and try to memorize the promises of God. Then, when you find yourself in a difficult situation, God will be able to comfort you with His promises as He brings them to mind. Here are some to start with: Deuteronomy 31:6; Matthew 10:18-20; Philippians 4:19.

No. 3: Be Holy

We all have a contribution to make to society. Some choose to delight in perverse and evil things. A child of God will, by the guidance of the Holy Spirit, choose to live righteously. "For it is written: 'Be holy, because I am holy' " (1 Peter 1:16).

So how do we live holy lives? Paul wrote: "Finally, brothers, whatever is true, whatever is noble, whatever is right, whatever is pure, whatever is lovely, whatever is admirable—if anything is excellent or praiseworthy—think about such things" (Philippians 4:8).

What we think often shows up in how we act. As your desire for things that are good increases, you're likely to want to distance yourself from video games, movies, TV shows and music that glorify evil things. Examine your life and ask God to show you what evil influences you need to turn away from, and do your part to add good to our world.

No. 4: Live the Life

If you're professing a faith in Jesus Christ as your Savior with your lips, hopefully it also will be demonstrated in your actions. When everything around you seems to be falling apart, remember the rock your faith is built on. Don't doubt. Don't waver. God is your God, and He will give you all that you need to remain firm in your faith. "Now it is God who makes both us and you stand firm in Christ" (2 Corinthians 1:21).

No. 5: Trust

Jesus said, "Do not let your hearts be troubled. Trust in God; trust also in me" (John 14:1). If there's anything we can do in the midst of evil, it's trust in God. He's been around for all that's ever happened. Every death, every war, every sneaky attack Satan's made. And God's still around. We sometimes wonder what He's doing. We don't always understand His tactics. We question how He'll possibly be able to redeem a horrible situation. But He does it every day. God is always working for good. We need to always be trusting Him to do that.

A Real Opportunity

So now that you're back in school, trying to live your life for God, why don't you participate in the annual "See You At The Pole" event? On a specific day in September, every year, millions of students around the world will gather at their campus flagpoles to pray for their schools, their countries and the world. You can play an important role in combating evil just by standing side by side with other students and lifting up a prayer to your heavenly Father.

Tell your school administration what you plan to do and then publicize the time and place for prayer. Many students will be meeting at their local time of 7 a.m. "See You At The Pole" is not a demonstration. It's completely legal. Check out the "See You At The Pole" Web site at www.syatp.com for answers to your questions. And remember: Be courageous! God commands it (Joshua 1:5-9). Great and mighty is the power of God within you—much more powerful than anything else in the world!

Dear Susie:

I saw an old guy friend of mine recently, and we've started talking and hanging out together. I want to be his friend—and I enjoy his friendship—but I don't think I'm ready for the "boyfriend girlfriend" scene yet. I just don't think he'll understand, and I'm not sure how to tell him. He's not a Christian, either. A little voice inside me is saying go with the flow, and another voice is telling me to hold back. I'm so confused! What should I do?

Becca

Dear Becca:

I admire your honesty and your tender heart. I'm also proud of you for wanting to take things slowly. This guy might *not* understand about simply being friends. But you'll never know until you talk about it.

There's another issue that I'd like to chat with you about, though. And that's the fact that he's not a Christian. That "little voice" inside of you that's causing you to be cautious is the Holy Spirit. God uses His Spirit within us to guide us in the way He wants us to go.

The tug you're feeling to "go with the flow" is a normal human desire—but it's a desire of the flesh, not of the Spirit. I believe God desires that we establish our strongest friendships with other Christians.

Am I saying not to befriend nonbelievers? Absolutely not! How will they ever see Jesus in our lives if we don't reach out to them? But there's a difference in reach out and being friendly and in establishing an intimate relationship.

My advice? You're eventually going to have to talk this out with him. Express your desire to remain friends and save your dating relationships for guys who share your faith and values.

Dear Susie:

I have a friend who's really tender-hearted. I mean, she'll see a crippled dog and start crying. And when someone new comes to school, she always tells me we should try to make friends with her. I don't know . . . I'm just not that outgoing. But she keeps pushing me on this.

Help!
Kimberly

Dear Kimberly:

Sounds like you're afraid to get out of your comfort zone. I admire your friend's willingness to befriend new students. It doesn't sound as if she's asking you to do this by yourself. Why couldn't you *together* reach out more to those around you?

There are definitely hundreds of lonely, hurting students

right inside your school who could use a Christian influence and a smile.

I suggest you talk to God about it

God Said...I Said

This is a private conversation.
DON'T READ...unless you
enjoy eavesdropping.

God Said: What about Julianna?

> I Said: What about her?

Why does she always
eat lunch alone?

> I don't know.

Have you ever thought it?

> Not really.

Why not?

> Well, that's just her.
> I mean . . . she *always* eats alone.
> I guess I'm just used to seeing
> her in the school cafeteria by herself.

Hmmm.

> It's no big deal. She probably likes it.

Would *you* like it?

> No way! I'm too much of a
> people-person to hang out
> by myself at lunch time!

Yet you'd have to . . .
if no one chose to sit with you.

> Whaddya mean if no one chose
> to sit with me? I've always got
> a *few* friends I can count on!

But what if you didn't?

> C'mon, God.
> What are You getting at?

Think about it: What if
you really *wanted* to be
with people, but you couldn't
find anyone to sit with you at lunch?

"An anxious heart weighs a man down, but a KIND WORD CHEERS him up."

(Proverbs 12:25)

No one?

No one.

Well, that'd be pretty tough. I mean . . . I . . . I'd really be hurting inside. I'd probably go home and cry every day.

Good.

Good?!?

Good—now you're thinking outside of yourself.

Whaddya mean?

You're imagining how someone else might feel if she were all alone but didn't really want to be.

You mean . . . Julianna?

Right.

Well, that's different. She's different.

How is she different?

Well, for one thing, she's always alone.

I thought we already covered this.

Well, what are You trying to say, God?

Okay. Yes, she's alone. We've already established that fact. But could it be that she doesn't really want to be alone?

I don't know. I just always assumed she wanted it that way or she'd do something about it.

Hmmm. Remember when you first started riding the bus to school?

Yeah. That was third grade.

Right.

So?

You didn't know anyone
on the bus. You sat with a
different kid every day—
hoping to make a friend—
but they ignored you simply
because you were the new "bus kid."

> I forgot all about that.
> Man! That was really a hard year.

Yes, it was . . .
until February.

> February?

It was February 3 that your
older sister asked her friend
Julie to consider *not* driving
her little sister, Marcie, to school.
She knew that you and Marcie
were good friends and if Marcie
would ride the bus with you,
you'd be more comfortable.

> Hey! I never knew
> Lindsey did that!

She loves you.

> Lindsey asked Julie to
> encourage Marcie to ride my bus?

That's right. And since
you only lived three blocks
away from each other, Lindsey
knew you'd both have the same route.

> Wow. I'm really glad
> Lindsey did that, because
> Marcie and I had a great
> time on the bus! It felt
> soooo good to finally have
> a friend to ride with me—
> you know—someone to
> laugh with, talk with, *be* with.

Now back to Julianna.

> Well, I don't ride the bus any more.

I know. But the same
principle is at work here.

> You've lost me, God.

Think about it. You really
wanted someone to sit with
 on the bus. But it never

happened until someone else
stepped in and helped you
with the friendship you needed.

Yeah.

So never assume just because
someone's alone that it's their
choice. Maybe Julianna doesn't
know *how* to do anything about it.
If you needed help, maybe she
could use some help, too.

Okay, so what are
You saying, God?
Give it to me straight.

I want you to eat lunch with her.

You're kidding, right?

No. I was kidding when I gave
the hyenas laughter. But I'm not
kidding about Julianna needing a friend.

But what about
my friends?

What about them?

I can't just leave them!

I didn't ask you to.

But You want me to eat lunch
with Julianna! How can I just
ignore my friends—the girls
I eat with every single day—
to go sit with a loner?

You don't have to leave them.
Invite Julianna to eat at *your* table.

Oh, man!

Remember how hurt you
were back in third grade?

Yeah.

Julianna's hurting, My child.
I care about her.
I need *you* to reach out to her.

But what'll I say?

Don't worry about that.
I'll give you the words.

And what if she
turns me down?

Don't worry about that, either.
I've already started preparing her heart.

What do You mean?

Well . . . she's been
praying for a friend.

You're kidding?!!

No. That was the hyenas, remember?

Oh, yeah.
But God . . .
You mean . . .
she's a Christian?

That's right. And she's been
praying for three months that
I'd help her find another
Christian friend at this school.

Wow. I never knew.

I've been trying to speak to You.

You mean . . . all that
stuff my youth leader's
been saying about bringing
someone to church?

Yes.

And loving someone new?

Yes.

And those Sunday school
lessons on not excluding others?

Yes.

And Mom asking me if
I've made any new
friends this year?

Yes.

Man! I sure am hard-headed
sometimes. I'm sorry, Father.
All this time, I've been praying
that You'd use me in a special
way this year at school. And
Julianna's been right under
my nose the whole time! Why
didn't I think of this on my own?

You were praying for an
opportunity . . . but you
weren't looking for an
opportunity. There's a difference.

Yeah! A big difference.

When you ask Me to
use you, always expect that
I'll bring an opportunity
your way to do just that.

Father, I *want* to be used.

I *want* You to make a difference through me.

I know, My child.

I will. But you've got to make the first move. YOU reach out . . . and trust ME to do the rest.

Father, will You forgive me for being so blinded to the needs of those around me? I'm really sorry.

You're forgiven. And with a tender heart like that, I can use you in numerous ways this year.

Thanks, Father. I gotta go now.

Where are you going?

I'm gonna call Amber and Kelli and Emily and Kristine and remind them that You want to use us to make a difference in Julianna's life.

Great! I'll come with you.

"Dear friends, let us LOVE ONE ANOTHER, for love comes from God."
(1 John 4:7)

Dear Susie:

I have a friend who's not very happy. She's threatened suicide before. I don't really think she'd go through with it, but I care about her and want to help. She just keeps saying that no one understands. Any ideas?

Meredith

Dear Meredith:

Suicide threats are nothing to ignore or mess around with. Let your friend know that you're extremely concerned that she's making such disturbing statements.

Probably the worst feeling in the world is not being understood by those around us, so I really feel for your friend. Please remind her, though, that Jesus reallyreallyreally *does* understand! He knows exactly how she feels and what she's going through.

Your friend needs you to be "Jesus with skin on." Can you do that? Will you ask God to help you love her as He Himself loves her? Don't be afraid to put your arm around her shoulders. Hug her. Send her encouraging notes.

There's probably a *reason* she's feeling no one understands. Ask her:

"Is it because you haven't *tried* communicating with anyone?" When we're depressed, it's often tempting to stuff our feelings deep inside.

"Maybe you *have* tried communicating your hurt, but haven't communicated it effectively. Are you trying to share your thoughts and feelings when you're angry? Are you really saying what you mean? Are you beating around the bush, making people try to guess what's bothering you?"

Encourage her to keep *trying* to communicate with those around her until she finds someone who will listen and understand. Remind her that you're more than willing to be that person for her. But also know that she might need some counseling. After all, you don't know what she's struggling with, and if she's threatening suicide, that's too big for you to handle on your own!